The Weather in the Imagination

The Weather in the Imagination

LUCIAN BOIA

Translated by Roger Leverdier

REAKTION BOOKS

Published by REAKTION BOOKS LTD
79 Farringdon Road
London EC1M 3JU, UK

www.reaktionbooks.co.uk

First published 2005
Copyright © Lucian Boia, 2005

English-language translation © Reaktion Books 2005

Printed and bound in Great Britain
by Biddles Ltd, King's Lynn

British Library Cataloguing in Publication Data
    Boia, Lucian
    The weather in the imagination
    1. Weather - Psychological aspects 2. Weather - Physiological
    effect 3. Climate and civilization
    I. Title
    304.2'5
    ISBN 1 86189 214 4

Contents

Introduction

What is happening to the weather? The third millennium is beginning with bad news: the climate seems to have become completely unsettled. Some people are already predicting the worst, claiming that the current rise in temperature threatens to seriously disrupt our life on the planet. Even if we are not quite witnessing the end of the world, we may see at least the collapse of our hubristic and reckless technological civilization? Man believed he could dominate Nature and bend it to his will, but Nature is now turning against him and he finds himself caught in a trap.

The above is no more than a scenario. The potential future, one we can only imagine, and the real future, whatever that may be, are two distinct – and often radically distinct – things. A mischievous person might make the point that prophecies and predictions (including those based on irrefutable scientific data) have almost always been invalidated by the way the world has actually developed.

Nobody can deny that climate is a massive, inescapable presence. Life itself originated and evolved within clearly defined climatic limits. That is why there are Earthlings, but no Martians. It is because of factors closely related to climate that the Mediterranean became the cradle of so many civilizations while

Antarctica is the realm of the penguins. Nor does technological man – at least now and for the foreseeable future – seem capable of freeing himself from the constraints of the natural world and inventing a completely 'artificial' civilization. From time to time, a big storm or a disastrous flood gives us a lesson in modesty and reminds us that we are still dependent on Mother Nature.

These are sensible but very general observations. Things become complicated as soon as we begin to examine more closely the mechanism linking climate and humanity: in other words, when we attempt to define the way climate actually affects past, present and future. There are a huge number of often contradictory interpretations, for while there is only one reality, there are many ways of looking at it. We should not confuse even the simplest object with its image or representation. Moreover, we should be particularly careful to distinguish between the complex movements and structures of nature and those of society. Reality is not simply absorbed by the human mind; it can only be adapted and is inevitably forced to obey the rules of the game.

By the 'rules of the game' I mean that our judgement is not entirely free. It is subject to many constraints because we are in some way programmed to see things in a certain way. The constants and variables of the human mind stand between the external world and our representations and interpretations of it.

Two types of mental constants seem particularly characteristic. First of all, the very human aptitude for perceiving differences rather than similarities; anything that more or less clashes with the norm is likely to attract our attention. The exception thus tends to obscure ordinary facts, although these are probably more essential. Certain features, chosen because of their 'impact', are isolated and exaggerated; by insisting on their unique aspect, we endow them with more importance than they actually deserve. We only have to study history or follow the news to note this penchant for anything that 'stands out'. (This is how the many distortions of the 'other' that have fostered racism and nationalism are created.)

The second constant is the human mind's craving for coherence. We aspire to inhabit a meaningful universe in which everything is contained within closed and intelligible systems. First magic, then religion, and finally philosophy, science and ideology has each in its own fashion done no more than invest the universe, history and human destiny with a determined meaning and the maximum possible coherence. But the result of this thirst for certainty has its paradox: our pursuit of the Absolute has led to a proliferation of solutions. Instead of one great Truth, we are now confronted with a frequently bewildering variety of so-called truths.

It is obvious that interpretations change as our knowledge of the world increases. But scientific progress does not explain everything. Human knowledge used to increase from one era to the next; nowadays it does so year by year. Even so, at every stage, divergent theories are constructed from the same stock of knowledge. Our image of the world is affected by a multitude of historical, social and cultural variables. All theories and opinions are dated and spatially and socially circumscribed. The scientific thinking that has conquered the world over the last few hundred years is a product of the West: it would have been quite a different story if we had opted for Chinese or Indian science, products of quite different philosophies. The real world is inevitably filtered through a Western cultural heritage. Moreover, in this context, it is highly dependent on ideologies, i.e., on the most influential values and beliefs held by a community. Nobody looks at things in a cool, objective way; every point of view is derived (consciously or unconsciously) from a vision of the world and forms part of a social programme.

We shall see what happens when these considerations are applied to climatic theories and the anxieties aroused by climate.

We should begin by noting the prominence given to the actual facts of climate and their more unusual manifestations. The weather has always been a traditional topic of conversation; it is probably the most common dialogue between human beings. But even at this perfectly banal everyday level, there are indications that it is regarded with suspicion. It would seem that it is always warmer or colder than usual, or it rains too much or too little (in relation to a standard that exists only as a result of these so-called deviations). Moreover, we have a tendency to dramatize the greater differences that may be observed from one region of the globe to another or from one historical period to another. It is quite obvious that some climates are harsher than others. The history of humanity is also punctuated by disasters attributable to climatic excesses. It is a paradox that, despite our dread of this or that climate, we generally adapt to it remarkably well. Of all the evolved life forms on the planet, only man has the ability to settle in any kind of climate and make himself at home. In the final analysis, the relationship between man and climate, shaped by human ingenuity and adaptability, turns out to be much more constructive than a climatic imagination fascinated by drama and spectacle would have us believe.

On the other hand, the need for coherence and the tendency to unify cosmic and human phenomena ensures climate's position as one of the great explanatory principles of human evolution. This is entirely understandable given its omnipresence. A history centred on climate is just as legitimate (and obviously just as disputable) as the religious determinism of St Augustine or Marx's economic determinism.

When we examine cultural and ideological trends we find that they offer every imaginable combination. It is no secret that modern-day prophets of climatic disaster do not believe in the virtues of technological civilization. Technophiles contest their claims with equal vehemence. Environmentalists versus liberals: both sides manipulate the same scientific data but use it in the service of opposing ideologies. Moreover, their scenarios derive from vast and long-established historical models. On the one hand stands progress, one of the great religions of the last few centuries. On the other, the spectre of decline, which harks back to the ancient view of history as a cyclical process, a rotation of ascension and collapse marked by a profusion of catastrophes, such as the Flood. Noting the cultural and ideological weight of every option is not a matter of automatically passing judgement on the truth or non-truth of the theory in question. Both optimists and pessimists may be right or wrong (or partially right or partially wrong) independently of their ideological reasons. But these reasons exist, and they offer us a grid for interpreting nature that enables us to resist a naïve infatuation with one cause or another.

The theories, scenarios and psychoses based on climate are distinguished by an inexhaustible diversity. We can, however, organize them into three main categories.

The first is *anthropological* and *psychological*; climate has long served as a means of explaining human diversity. Early travellers, historians and geographers were struck by a double contrast: the diversity of landscape and the diversity of human beings and peoples. How could they resist the temptation to explain the one by the other? Human beings are different because they live under different skies. The climatic interpretation of racial, ethnic and cultural particularities (from physical anthropology to the psychology of peoples or the 'character of nations', as David Hume put it) runs through the philosophy of history and culture from antiquity to the relatively recent past.

The second category is *historical*: climate as a way of illuminating the progress of history. It is called on to explain the dynamic of the historical process, its development and decline, the rise of certain civilizations and the stagnation or regression of others. This dynamic interpretation of the relation between climate and history was also initiated during antiquity but not applied systematically until history began to be seen as an evolutionary process. The eighteenth and nineteenth centuries were influenced by the double theory of progress and evolution and also by the extraordinary advances the West had achieved in comparison with other parts of the world. They tended to regard climate as one of the causal factors (sometimes even the primary factor) in the historical development and the radically different destinies of civilizations.

The third category combines *climate* and *catastrophe*. This excessively over-dramatized view is also embedded in the great models of history. What could destroy a civilization – or arouse the fear of humanity's total extinction – more effectively than a good climatic 'jolt'? The prototype of this kind of upheaval is the Flood, one of the most gripping and influential myths the human imagination has ever produced. The Flood is the symbol of a history punctuated by 'ends of the world' (which are usually incomplete and almost always allow a small group of survivors to begin another cycle). At first, the Flood and similar disasters formed part of the arsenal of the forces of divine justice. As time went on, they came to be regarded as strictly natural phenomena. In our own day, they are generally considered the perverse effects – unexpected but 'deserved' – of our abuse of the natural world. The logic of sin and its punishment remains intact but the meaning changes. The traditional Flood was caused by the sins of men against God. The future Flood may be triggered by their sins against Nature. Over the course of the last century, this anxiety has been maintained in the form of a preoccupation with the 'end of civilization', a radical contrast to the optimists' theory of continuous and relatively risk-free progress. It is apposite that research into climate history has revealed not just the variability of climate through the ages but also its volatility. The malfunctioning of technological civilization and the fragility of climate are inseparably linked in the key concept of global warming (due, as we know, to the pollution resulting from human activity). According to the direst predictions, it will not be long before the earth is almost uninhabitable or, at the very least, incapable of sustaining a highly developed civilization.

It is not for the author of this book to take sides in the current debate about climate, to affirm or question, exaggerate or play down global warming and its consequences. I can only admire those who already know what the future holds. For my part, I have no idea. But another story, related yet separate, runs parallel with the 'true' story of climate and its future: the story of a human imagination that has been stimulated and sometimes even inflamed by climatic phenomena. This is the story I propose to tell.

ONE

Climate and People

A POET LOST IN THE SNOW

We can begin our subject in a thousand different ways. Where can we find the most suitable example? For fictional representations of climate, the verse reportages of Ovid seem to offer an appropriate point of departure. In AD 8 the poet, once the idol of Rome's worldly society, was condemned to exile by the emperor Augustus for reasons that remain mysterious. He was forced to spend the last ten years of his life in Tomis (now the Romanian city of Constanta), a former Greek colony on the shores of the Black Sea. His last two collections of poems, *Tristia* and *Ex Ponto*, are cries of distress. They depict the savagery of men and places: Tomis, a remote bastion of Greek civilization, was surrounded by Getes and Scythians, alien tribes who burst into mocking laughter whenever they heard Latin spoken. And there was also the climate, a far cry from the mildness of the Mediterranean. It was cold, terribly cold:

> The snow lies continuously, and once fallen, neither sun nor rains may melt it … So when an earlier fall is not yet melted another has come, and in many places 'tis wont to remain for two years . . . With skins and stitched breeches they keep out the evils of the cold; of the whole body only the face is

exposed. Often their hair tinkles with hanging ice and their beards glisten white with the mantle of frost. Exposed wine stands upright, retaining the shape of the jar, and they drink, not draughts of wine but fragments served them . . . The very Hister [the Danube] . . . freezes as the wind stiffens his dark flood, and winds its way into the sea with covered waters. Where ships had gone before now men go on foot, and the waters congealed with cold feel the hoof-beat of the horse . . . I have seen the vast sea stiff with ice, a slippery shell holding the water motionless. And seeing is not enough; I have trodden the frozen sea, and the surface lay beneath an unwetted foot . . . [1]

This is an arctic landscape painted by a poet turned polar explorer. The inhabitants eat their wine and the snow lasts from one winter to the next. Little matter if these things occurred on a latitude well below the polar circle. Today the Black Sea beaches are famous for their warmth in summer, although the continental climate does indeed produce hard winters. At a pinch we might concede that the climate was a little colder in Ovid's day. Moreover, even in more recent periods the Danube frequently used to freeze in winter, forming a bridge of ice. But it is certain that the ice would soon have melted completely under the rays of the spring sun.

The unhappy exile was undoubtedly indulging in poetic licence in the hope of softening hearts in Rome. Even so, his verse expressed a coherent view of how the world was struc-tured. Ovid was banished to the north-east corner of the Empire, close to the final frontier. Beyond the mouths of the Danube lay the vague and unexplored territory of the 'Great North'. Normality, in climate as in everything else, was obviously specific to the centre. The periphery, on the other hand, was a place where distortions of human nature were associated with climatic excess.

Ovid's description of an eternally cold world owes more to ideology than to observation. Do we accept the evidence of our eyes or do we see what we are supposed to see? Ovid addressed an audience that was likely to accept his word because its culture was impregnated with a significantly dramatized and ideologically coloured image of the world.

EXTREMES OF COLD AND HEAT

Diodorus of Sicily, whose *Bibliotheca Historica* appeared some decades before Ovid's time, was a meticulous scholar rather than a poet and drew his information from the best available sources. For him, climatic extremes were illustrated by the contrast between the Scythian territories to the north of the Black Sea and the land of the Troglodytes to the south of Egypt:

> So great, for instance, is the contrast between our climate and the climates which we have described that the difference, when considered in detail, surpasses belief. For example, there are countries where, because of the excessive cold, the greatest rivers are frozen over, the ice sustaining the crossing of armies and the passage of heavily laden wagons, the wine and all the other juices freeze so that they must be cut with knives, yea, what is more wonderful still, the extremities of human beings fall off when rubbed by their clothing, their eyes are blinded, fire furnishes no protection, even bronze statues are cracked open . . . [2]

Although these bizarre phenomena were occurring just north of the Black Sea, well below where Moscow or St Petersburg stand today, the far south was equally uncomfortable:

But on the furthermost bounds of Egypt and the Troglodyte country, because of the excessive heat from the sun at midday, men who are standing side by side are unable even to see one another because of the thickness of the air as it is condensed, and no one can walk about without any foot-gear, since blisters appear at once on any who go barefoot. And as for drink, unless it is ready to hand to satisfy the need of it, they speedily perish, since the heat swiftly exhausts the natural moistures in the body. Moreover, whenever any man puts any food into a bronze vessel along with water and sits it in the sun, it quickly boils without fire or wood . . . [3]

Apparently, it was only possible to enjoy a drink in Rome or Greece; at higher or lower latitudes, the liquid was likely to freeze or to evaporate!

The dominant theory of climate during antiquity was the 'five zones' theory attributed to the Greek philosopher Parmenides (fifth century BC).[4] Between each of the Earth's poles a frigid zone gave way to a temperate zone, both of which bordered a central torrid zone. At first sight, this seems to conform to reality in that it reflects existing climatic conditions. But the disparities were exaggerated: the alignment clearly separated normality from abnormality. According to the ancients, once the climate was hot or cold, it stayed that way forever. The temperate zone, the only one inhabitable in practical terms, corresponded in most respects to Greco-Roman territory (the Mediterranean area). A little further to the north or south, you found yourself in the midst of a climatic disaster (and as we have just learned from Ovid, things were already beginning to take a turn for the worse on the Empire's frontiers).

A brief word on terminology is needed at this point. In Classical Greek, *climate* meant *inclination*, an association that does not exist in modern languages.[5] The word defined the inclination of the Earth's axis on the plane of the horizon; the angle thus formed corresponded with the latitude of each area. In short, 'climate' was virtually synonymous with 'latitude'. We express this in degrees; Greek scholars expressed it by the length of the day at the time of the solstice. Thus the climate at noon was located on the equator, where day and night are always of equal length. It gradually increased towards the north, becoming 17.00 hours in Ireland (at 54°). The system offered variants; climates, i.e., degrees of latitude, could be counted by differences of 60, 30 or 15 minutes.

The actual meaning of the word 'climate' was expressed through the word 'zone', which meant 'belt'. The Earth was circumscribed by 'zones', bands lying between parallel circles and characterized by specific climatic conditions. These conditions obviously varied in relation to latitude. Thus by a quite logical process of semantic slippage, the word climate came to acquire the meaning we give it today.

The prevailing scientific mentality and the general conception of how the world was structured differed from our own as much as did the terminology. The Classical world mixed geometry with climatology and science with a magical conception of the universe. It believed in a perfect correlation between the terrestrial sphere and the heavens. The zones and parallels it traced around the globe resulted from the projection of celestial zones and parallels. There were many correspondences between our world and the celestial canopy. This cosmic harmony prefigured and would go on to justify astrological interpretations.

Let us return to the 'zones' and more particularly to questions of 'heat' and 'cold'. Strabo, the greatest geographer of antiquity, developed the theory of the five zones at length in his *Geographica*. His complicated calculations are an attempt to define the extent of the uninhabited territories around the equator and to the north of the Scythian lands (modern Ukraine) and the British Isles; the 54th parallel seemed to mark the limit of human habitation. Ovid shared the same conviction. The first song of *Metamorphoses* (one of the most widely read texts of world literature) recounts the genesis of the Earth and mankind. The author makes it clear that climatic conditions in the hot and cold zones are too extreme to support human life.

There were exceptions to the rule, however. The Hyperboreans, located somewhere in the far north, did not live amid perpetual snows but, curiously, enjoyed a constantly mild climate. India, situated at the eastern tip of the known world, was distinguished by a wide range of climatic anomalies. Curtius Rufus, a Latin historian of the first century AD, believed that the seasons were reversed in India: when it was hot in the Mediterranean, it was snowing there. According to the Greek author Ctesias (fifth century BC), India experienced no rainfall at all but was subject to extremely strong winds.[6]

The Greco-Roman cultural heritage enjoyed immense prestige until the middle of the modern period. The defining intellectual achievement of the Middle Ages was its fusion of Christian theology and Classical learning. The Renaissance believed it was somehow reprising or 'recreating' the intellectual and artistic feats of the Classical world. Even towards 1700, when the march of modernity was in full stride, the dispute between the so-called 'Ancients' and 'Moderns' in France and in Britain demonstrated that defenders of the superiority of the ancient world had not yet given up. For a long time, Western civilization had been unaware that it was creating something entirely new. Yet the West was to discover – and later to conquer and exploit – every corner of the globe. The Greeks, the Romans and other traditional civilizations had proved incapable of breaking free from their own intellectual constructs. But respect for antiquity was so great that theorists and even explorers still preferred the abstract and often fantastical schemas of Greek writers, dead for two thousand years, to the evidence of their own eyes. Columbus refused to accept the existence of America because it did not feature on the Greeks' imaginary map of the world. For centuries, explorers set out to locate the great Austral continent simply because, unlike America, it *did* figure on imaginary maps. (James Cook's Pacific voyages finally gave this tenacious myth the *coup de grace*.)

This attitude extended to the climatic zones. John Holywood, a thirteenth-century English mathematician better known by the Latinized name Sacrobosco, wrote a highly respected treatise, *De Sphaera Mundi*, in which he re-examined the zone system as interpreted by Ptolemy and other Greco-Roman authorities. Holywood, like his predecessors, adamantly maintained the impossibility of inhabiting the Arctic regions and the Torrid Zone. Such ideas were still prevalent in the fifteenth century. Theorists stuck to their guns while rumours circulated about ships swallowed by the boiling seas off the African coast, although some Portuguese navigators had already passed the critical line. In 1434, Gil Eannes sailed past Cape Bojador, on the Saharan coast at latitude 26°, once considered one of the world's terminal points. Scholars had to face the facts. By 1500, the zones theory, or at least its more dramatic elements, had had its day.[7] The idea was emerging that man could settle in any part of the world and adapt to any climate.

DIFFERENT CLIMATES, DIFFERENT PEOPLE, DIFFERENT HISTORIES

Uninhabitable zones were simply the extreme expression of a comprehensive system that brought together geographic, climatic and biological factors and arranged them progressively (and hierarchically) in a pattern linking the *centre* to the *periphery*. We all tend to feel that the world revolves around us. Every individual and every human community looks at the universe from a central position. Others are judged in relation to the values of the individual or the group. A somewhat attenuated form of this attitude persists today, in a multicultural context where the constant mingling of very different groups highlights the diversity and relative nature of values. In such a context, it is no longer 'politically correct' to create cultural hierarchies and disparage the 'other'. But the system of otherness functioned at full strength for millennia; it was the only way of coherently organizing a widely distributed and hierarchical humanity in which the 'other' was invested with markedly different traits.

However, while every ethnic group or human community has a centre, some are more equal than others. Their power, or the vitality of their civilization, or a combination of both, compels them to hegemonic aspirations; they are so convinced of their superiority that they succeed in imposing it – and a great many of their values – on territories far beyond their own frontiers. The United States naturally comes to mind as a contemporary example of this type of privileged position. But for many centuries China provided the absolute model of the 'centre'; moreover, it significantly referred to itself as the Middle Kingdom. The world beyond its frontiers was reduced to an infinite collection of geographical and human oddities. The Greeks devised a particularly rigorous and almost geometric distribution of the distinctive traits of human groups; increasingly accentuated levels of otherness led, stage by stage, from the absolute centre of normality (Greece, and Athens in particular) to the absolute abnormality that characterized the world's periphery. The greater the distance, the greater the difference.[8]

Anomalies could be adequately explained in terms of distance. But there was a great temptation to fuse the two series of distinctions: those concerning the environment, especially climate, and those relating to human diversity. The first rational, scientific system for interpreting biological and social phenomena (detached from strictly providential interpretations) was based on geographical determinism, the original and most durable of the philosophies of history. What could, at first, sight be more obvious? Human beings are different and they live in different environments. If we change one word we arrive at: 'Human beings are different because they live in different environments.'

Histories are different, too. Every human group evolves in its own way and civilizations are striking in their diversity. This multitude of historical trajectories can apparently be explained by the double diversity of men and environments. But just as men are different because environments differ, the entire historical process is ultimately determined by geographical diversity.

Climate is indisputably the most powerful and influential of all environmental factors; thus geographical determinism appears in the first instance as a climatic determinism. We now tend to dismiss such thinking as simplistic and reactionary. But for many centuries it was the only theory that offered a *natural* interpretation of human diversity: already, long before the advent of Lamarck and Darwin, the idea of adaptability to environmental conditions seemed to herald, if not quite evolutionism, at least a certain idea of the variety of the species.

Why were the Egyptians so different from the Greeks, indeed from all other peoples? Herodotus knew the answer and stated it explicitly: 'In keeping with the idiosyncratic climate which prevails there and the fact that their river behaves differently from any other river, almost all Egyptian customs and practices are the opposite of those of everywhere else.'[9]

Hippocrates (*c.* 460–377 BC), the most famous doctor of antiquity, sketched the first general system of climatic interpretation in his treatise *Airs, Waters, Places*. He posited a fundamental climatic distinction between Europe and Asia. (By Asia we should understand only the part of that vast continent known to the Greeks – the Middle East, Mesopotamia, Persia and, more vaguely, India.) Europe faces north and west but Asia faces south and east. Equidistant from cold and warmth, its lands enjoy a mild and rather balanced climate: the region 'is not burnt up with the heat nor dried up by drought and want of water, it is not oppressed with cold, nor yet damp with excessive rains and snow'. Hippocrates paints a picture of perpetual spring, but there are drawbacks. Uniformity of climate is responsible for a certain uniformity in the nature of humanity – Asians look alike. Moreover, the spring-like mildness does nothing to stimulate energy. 'Courage, endurance, industry and high spirit could not arise in such conditions either among the natives or among immigrants'.[10]

Europe, on the other hand, is marked by distinct seasonal variations:

the changes of the season . . . are violent and frequent, while there are severe heatwaves, severe winters, copious rains and then long droughts, and winds, causing many changes of various kinds. Wherefore, it is natural to realize that generation too varies in the coagulation of the seed, and is not the same for the same seed in summer as in winter nor in rain as in drought.[11]

The difference between individuals, peoples and communities is more pronounced in Europe than it is in Asia. Hippocrates provides an inventory of regional differences: mountain dwellers are tall, courageous and industrious; those who live in grassland valleys, where the hot winds blow, are short, stocky, far more timid and display little inclination for work. There is much more in this vein; each environment has its representative human type.[12] Despite this inexhaustible variety, most European peoples, stimulated by climatic 'jolts', are more courageous and freedom-loving than Asians. It is easy to understand why they are more suited to Greek-style democracy, for Asian despotism has an impartial ally in the gentle and submissive nature of its subjects. This 'explains' the ease with which Alexander the Great conquered the Persian Empire: how could the 'soft' Asian character resist the energy of Europe?

Moving away from temperate climate (uniform in Asia and contrasting in Europe), we find that more distant regions are dominated by cold or heat. Hippocrates lingers over descriptions of climatic conditions in the Scythian lands:

> A thick fog envelops by day the plains upon which they live, so that winter is perennial, while summer, which is but feeble, lasts only a few days . . . And the changes of the seasons are neither great nor violent, the seasons being uniform and altering but little. Wherefore the men also are like one another in physique, since summer and winter they always use similar food and the same clothing, breathing a moist, thick atmosphere, drinking water from ice and snow, and abstaining from fatigue.[13]

The warmth and dryness of the Egyptian climate are cited in contrast to Scythian rain and cold. In both cases, as in Asia, the result is human uniformity. Asia represents spring, Egypt summer and Scythia winter, while Europe benefits from a complete succession of seasons, and this is the source of its diversity.

Climatic excesses are more powerful than human nature. Apparently, cold fostered barbarity. According to the third-century author Solinus, 'the customs of the peoples of the Scythian interior are rather fierce: they live in caves and drink from skulls . . . they drink the blood of the dead by sucking their wounds.' In one of these tribes, 'the custom is to sing at family funerals. They invite their friends and rend the corpses with their teeth, and make meals of the strips of flesh, which they mix with the flesh of animals. As for the skulls, they decorate them with gold and use them as drinking vessels.'[14] Remarkably, in the same region one sometimes comes across a tribe that practices vegetarianism and the whole range of virtues. As this perfection is located so far from the equitable environment enjoyed by the Greeks, it is just as suspect as the savagery of other tribes. The excellent Hyperboreans, paragons of virtue and happiness, are beyond further consideration: they are so remote – inhabiting the 'absolute' end of the world – that they seem completely detached from all systems of climatic or historical logic.

To the west, the British Isles, situated on the same latitude as Scythia, offered a similar climatic and human picture. Curiously, Strabo placed Ireland (*Ierne*) to the north of Britain, making it the last outpost of humanity. But what humanity! The Britons were distinguished by their barbarity, but the Irish were even worse, being both herbivorous and cannibalistic (the two extremes of alimentary otherness brought together). They considered it both a duty and a pleasure to eat their dead kin. An unbridled sexual promiscuity completes the picture: all women were fair game to the men, including their own mothers and sisters.[15] There was nothing to be done – it was all the climate's fault.

To the south, Egypt was doing well – it was a great civilization, after all. Even so, the Egyptians had their peculiarities; in some respects their behaviour was the total opposite of what was considered normal. Beyond Egypt's borders, nothing could withstand the ferocious African summer; the heat overwhelms and distorts everything. The African environment produces a series of monsters, creatures halfway between man and beast. Even in communities where the human aspect was more or less intact, there were still all kinds of characteristic moral and social deviations. The Troglodytes live in caves and feed on the flesh of snakes; they hiss instead of speaking. The Ichthyophagi go about completely naked and practice absolute communism, relegating their animals, women and children to common ownership. They live by the sea, in rocky clefts connected by a labyrinth of channels; they possess no weapons and eat nothing but fish. They suffer from total moral and intellectual confusion and make no distinction between honour and disgrace.[16] The sun had a lot to answer for. Despite these observations, the Ethiopians, like the Hyperboreans, are distinguished by their physical and moral perfection. At the 'absolute' ends of the world, myth is more powerful than climate.

Here I must make a point that holds true for the rest of this book. Nobody, not even the builders of theories (or so we may hope), is so narrow-minded as to claim that there is nothing outside the climate (or collective geographical factors). Human beings, individually or collectively, and history in its entirety, are stimulated by a multitude of factors. Even the most deterministic theories acknowledge this complexity, although they always presuppose a foundation on which to erect the entire theoretical edifice (we may make the analogy with the more recent theory advanced by Marx: his economic determinism acknowledges the relatively important and indeed autonomous role played by a variety of agents but everything is obliged to adapt to the economic base).

Thus Hippocrates, having set out his deterministic hypothesis, applied himself to adding nuances. Asians are as they are because of climate, yet 'their institutions are a contributory cause, the greater part of Asia being governed by kings'. Here, in fact, is an additional reason for their lack of audacity. On the other hand, 'All the inhabitants of Asia, whether Greek or non-Greek, who are not ruled by despots, but are independent, toiling for their own advantage, are the most warlike of all men.' Unlike the former, they have personal interests to defend.[17] We cannot cancel out climate but apparently we can come to some kind of accommodation with it.

Aristotle's *Politics* took the Hippocratic argument and developed it into a succinct, precise and 'definitive' interpretation that linked, climate, government and the psychology of peoples. With rigorous adaptations, this model was to endure until the middle of the modern scientific era, a span of two thousand years. According to Aristotle, the peoples of the north are courageous but their intelligence is limited; they thus possess an acute sense of freedom but little ability to organize politically and impose their will on others. Asians are more intelligent and creative, but because they lack courage and energy are condemned to servitude. The Greeks, situated between these two extremes, are blessed with good territorial and climatic conditions and combine the good qualities (apparently not the faults) of both worlds: they are intelligent and courageous, enjoy the best form of government and are capable, if they form a single state, of dominating the entire world.[18] This was actually about to happen: Aristotle's pupil, Alexander the Great, offered living proof that intellectual and moral superiority was climatically determined.

Paradoxically, it was Strabo, the most celebrated of the ancient world's geographers, who was most sceptical about the influence of the physical world on human development (it is fair to say that he had a better grasp of the subject than his peers). But he is not completely exempt from the penchant for determinism (an inevitable way of thinking at the time), and he also praises the climate and variety of forms particular to Europe. The part of the continent 'which is flat and has a temperate climate' seems to him to be most conducive to civilization. However, man can overcome the constraints of climate to the point of cancelling out its effects.

> Of the inhabitable part of Europe, the cold mountainous regions furnish by nature only a wretched existence to their inhabitants, yet even the regions of poverty and piracy become civilized as soon as they get good administrators. Take the case of the Greeks: though occupying mountains and rocks, they used to live happily, because they took fore-thought for good government, for the arts, and in general for the science of living. The Romans, too, took over many nations that were naturally savage owing to the regions they inhabited, because these regions were either rocky or without harbours or cold or for some reason ill-suited to habitation by many, and thus not only brought into communication with each other peoples who had been isolated but also taught the more savage how to live under forms of government.[19]

In other words, it is not so much Greece that made the Greeks but the Greeks who made Greece!

Here is another, more philosophical observation:

> And again, as regards the various arts and faculties and institutions of mankind, most of them, when once men have made a beginning, flourish in any latitude whatsoever and in certain instances even in spite of the latitude; so that some local

characteristics of a people come by nature, others by training and habit. For instance, it was not by nature that the Athenians were fond of letters, whereas the Lacedaemonians, and also the Thebans, who are still closer to the Athenians, were not so but rather by habit. So, also, the Babylonians and the Egyptians are philosophers, not by nature, but by training and habit. And further, the excellent qualities of horses, cattle, and other animals, are the result, not merely of locality, but of training also.[20]

Strabo's thinking is surprisingly modern; few works on climate contain such balanced remarks.

ARAB GEOGRAPHY

Europe remained closed to the outside world for much of the long period of the Middle Ages. The taste for distant adventures did not return until its final centuries, with the launching of the Crusades and the discovery of China. For a time, the Arabs led the geographical race. Their explorers and geographers considerably enlarged the space of the known and reported world but in the end produced a catalogue of 'otherness' rather similar to the one compiled by the Greeks. Like the Greeks and Romans, the Arabs placed themselves at the centre of the world, which meant that the centre of climatic and human normality shifted to the south.

It was generally believed by the Arabs at the time that most of the Earth's surface was uninhabited. Its inhabited areas were divided into seven climatic zones that traditionally extended from south to north (although a later interpretation arranged them in a circular pattern that ignored latitude). The fourth zone, location of the most favourable climate and the most highly developed civilization, comprised North Africa, Syria, Iraq and Persia. Baghdad was the absolute centre of the world.[21]

The further north or south the traveller ventured, the more human character altered. Human life assumed increasingly strange forms before disappearing completely. The European 'cold lands' were inhabited by the Slavic and Germanic peoples:

> As the sun, because of its distance, exerts only a feeble power over these regions, cold and humidity dominate and the snow and ice rarely melt. The humours there have little warmth. The men are tall, of wild character, coarse manners, low intelligence and heavy speech. Their complexion is so extraordinarily pale that it is almost blue. Their skin is fine and their flesh heavy; their eyes are blue and harmonize with the nuances of their complexion, and their long, loose hair is red through the effect of the humid vapours. Their religious beliefs are without solidity, owing to the nature of the cold and the lack of warmth.[22]

According to another account (the twelfth-century *Geography* of Edrisi, or al-Idrisi), Scotland was a wilderness devoid of towns, villages or dwellings; England was afflicted by a 'perpetual winter'; Norway, a sparsely populated 'island', was home to a race of forest-dwelling savages, while the inhabitants of the Baltic coast sought shelter in caves during the winter.[23]

These are curious and rather unflattering portraits of our European ancestors. Indeed – to paraphrase Montesquieu – given such conditions how was it possible to be European? The prevalence of ice and fog explain the lack of intelligence and the absence of religious sensibility. The effects of cold and humidity are severe, although perhaps less brutalizing than those inflicted by extremes of heat. This becomes clear when we turn our attention to the black races, apparently even less accomplished than their European counterparts!

To avoid getting lost in this maze of interpretations, it is best to turn to Ibn Khaldun, the most celebrated of Arab historians, who lived in the latter part of the fourteenth century. The *Introduction* (*Muqaddimah*) to his *Universal History* (1375–9), proposes climate as the first explicatory principle of human diversity, the second classic exposition of that theory, after Hippocrates. Ibn Khaldun returned to the seven-zone theory mentioned above: the fourth climate is the most balanced, while the third and the fifth, a little further to the south and north respectively, generally preserve the essential traits of normality. Civilizations cannot develop outside these three climates. It is only within their limits that people can construct houses and towns, practise their trades, engage in intellectual pursuits and acquire a sense of religion. This applies to Arabs in the first instance, followed by the Greeks and Byzantines, the Persians, the Israelites, the Indians and the Chinese.

Conversely, people living in extreme climates (the first and second zones encompassing central Africa and the sixth and seventh zones encompassing central and northern Europe) exist in a state of savagery: 'All their conditions are remote from those of human beings and close to those of wild animals.' Africans are particularly unfortunate: 'It has even been reported that most of the Negroes of the first zone dwell in caves and thickets; they eat herbs, live in savage isolation, do not congregate and eat one another.' The problem with this system is that the Arabs' own homeland, the Arabian Peninsula, lies within the two first climates – theoretically, it should be populated by savages! However, Ibn Khaldun claims exceptional circumstances: the sea that surrounds Arabia creates climatic conditions similar to those found in the central temperate zone.

Climate was also responsible for racial characteristics, particularly skin colour. Black peoples are black because of the sun and intense heat. Conversely, the peoples of the north are extremely pale. Ibn Khaldun does not believe in genetic fatality. When black people move to a cooler climate their descendants turn white, while white people settling in black territories will grow darker. Climate is more powerful than race or any form of genetic inheritance.[24]

However, Ibn Khaldun has a second interpretive approach that rivals the influence of climate. Differences between human communities may be explained by the way these communities obtain the materials necessary for their survival. Individuals form societies in order to work together to produce or adapt these materials. Does this sound familiar? It brings to mind the Marxist theory of production as the basis of all social construction. Ibn Khaldun's idea may seem like a precocious synthesis of Montesquieu, the first modern theorist of climatic influence, and Marx. But the two later thinkers owe him nothing; his work was not translated into European languages until the latter part of the nineteenth century (French editions appeared in 1858 and 1862).

JEAN BODIN: FRANCE AT THE CENTRE

The French philosopher Jean Bodin (1530–1596) provides the third classic text of geographical and climatic interpretation, after Hippocrates and Ibn Khaldun. His thinking is both traditional and typical of a new era, the Renaissance. 'Renaissance' signifies the recovery and adaptation of ancient models; Bodin's starting point is clearly the writings of Hippocrates and Aristotle. But the accomplishments of the era went far beyond intellectual preoccupations; it was a time of great geographical discoveries, an opening towards every part of the planet. Climatic theory had originally emerged from the Greeks' sense of wonder when confronted with the East. This time history repeated itself on a much greater scale: the proliferation of new landscapes and civilizations led the West to the realization that the two types of diversity – natural and cultural – were related. The Renaissance, seduced by the spirit of system and the possibility of uniting all phenomena in simple and comprehensive explanatory schemas, was also the era in which modern science took its first steps, although it remained attached to ancient science as well as to forms of 'parallel' knowledge like alchemy and astrology. The political spirit of the time saw theological precepts and Christian universalism begin to give way to the interests of the State and the principles of good government.

Bodin was primarily a political thinker. France was being torn apart by religious wars and he wanted to find the best type of political organization for his country. But laws and institutions do not constitute universal values; they have to be adapted to each cultural space and to the psychology of the peoples living in it. The psychology and behaviour of peoples are largely dependent on the environment in which they evolve. Bodin's theory of civilization centres on geographic and climatic determinism. The ideas are not new, nor are most of the arguments, but for the first time there is a rigorously argued, extremely detailed and virtually complete system. It explains everything; it is a wide-ranging and flawless interpretation of social and historical phenomena, as impressive as St Augustine's theological interpretation or the socio-economic theory of Marx. Bodin introduces it in *Méthode de l'histoire* (*Methodus ad Facilem Historiarum Cognitionem*, 1566) and develops it in *Les six livres de la République* (1576).[25]

Bodin first addresses the location of peoples according to degrees of latitude. Each hemisphere is divided into three major zones. From the equator to the thirtieth degree of latitude lie the hot regions inhabited by the southern peoples; from the thirtieth to the sixtieth degree, the temperate regions and the 'middle' peoples; from the sixtieth degree to the pole, the cold regions and the northern peoples. Bodin divides each of these three parts into two, resulting in segments of fifteen degrees each. Apart from the characteristics of its own zone, each sub-division is distinguished by traits related to the neighbouring region. Thus the 'middle' peoples, situated between 30 and 45 degrees, are more or less closely related to southerners, while those living between 45 and 60 degrees have much in common with northern peoples.

The peoples of the north are strong in body but less so in mind. Southerners are physically weaker but more ingenious. Consequently, the former are more active and more suited to manual labour and warfare, while the latter are more contemplative and more suited to the sciences, philosophy and religion. These noble preoccupations do not prevent them from showing a penchant for sex, which is far from the case in northern climes. Between these two extremes, the peoples of the temperate zone are stronger than southerners but less ingenious, and at the same time more cerebral but physically weaker than northerners. They have more talent for political activity and, in general, for anything that involves human interaction, e.g., administration, legislation, justice and commerce. Bodin lived at a time when astrology was the height of fashion and science had yet to detach itself from the traditional occult sciences. He was a contemporary of Nostradamus and used astrology to confirm his thesis. Astrology obliged: the north is dominated by Mars and the moon, which signify war and hunting; the south by Saturn and Venus, contemplation and love, and the middle region by Jupiter and Mercury, a combination appropriate to political governance. France, of course, is located at the very centre of the system; it synthesizes the qualities of north and south and endows them with its own political spirit and vocation for statehood. This represents a significant shift to the north in relation to the Greece of Hippocrates, not to mention the North Africa and Middle East of Ibn Khaldun. To each his centre . . .

The system brings everything into sharp relief. It was apparent that wars between France and England began with English victories and ended with peace terms favourable to the French. This intriguing paradox was entirely motivated by climate. The more northerly English were stronger and better at making war; the more southerly French possessed greater intelligence and negotiating skills. Moreover, the French advantage became a liability when the enemy was situated to the south. The same logic dictated that the French struggle against Spain would result in the latter winning the peace!

Bodin's work also incorporates an east–west opposition, although at the same time he points out that longitude is not responsible for differences to the same extent as latitude, i.e., climate in its most obvious manifestations. Even so, the peoples of the east have much in common with those of the south. They are gentler, more ingenious and less aggressive. Thus, 'the peoples of China, the most eastern of all peoples, are certainly the most ingenious of men and the most polite'. They may live on almost the same latitudes as Europe but their eastern position stamps them with distinctly southern characteristics. On the other hand, the west more closely resembles the north. The coarseness of northern peoples becomes more pronounced as it spreads westward and reaches its apogee in Brazil, whose peoples are 'the most barbarous and cruel'. The indigenous peoples of the New World were the objects of a myth-making process that defined them all, in the words of one contemporary observer, as 'naked, cruel and cannibalistic'.

Bodin refines and completes his system with further contrasts and geographical details and makes an important distinction between *mountain* and *plain*. Mountain-dwellers resemble the Nordic races, while the people of the plains resemble southerners. This allows for a variety of combinations, including some of those found within a single city. Why, for example, had Athens and

Rome suffered so much factionalism and civil disorder? Nobody had yet come up with an adequate explanation for these interminable confrontations. Bodin prides himself on having found the key to this enigma:

> In the same climate, latitude and longitude, and to the same degree, we may perceive the difference between the mountainous place and the plain, in such a way that in the same city, the diversity existing in high places and in valleys creates a variety of humours and also of manners, so that towns sited on uneven ground are more subject to sedition and change than those situated on even ground. Also the city of Rome, which has seven hills, was hardly ever without sedition.

As for Athens:

> There were three factions of diverse humours: those of the high city demanded the popular state; those of the lower town demanded an oligarchic state; and the inhabitants of the port of Piraeus desired an aristocratic state accommodating both nobility and the common people.

So there was an answer even for the contradiction between Athens and Thebes, very different cities despite their proximity and the fact that they shared the same latitude and environment. The cause, Bodin explains, must be sought in the orientation of the valleys: Athens is oriented towards the south, Thebes towards the north. The Athenians had therefore dedicated themselves to letters, science and arts while the Thebans had led a martial existence.

Other elements, more briefly considered, add to the validity of this imposing theoretical edifice. Winds may calm or arouse the passions. The fertility or sterility of the soil has its own effects; sterility in particular demands sobriety and hard work, as at Athens. Sea and islands shape behaviour: islanders are shrewder and slyer compared with mainland peoples; frontiers encourage cruel and warlike tendencies.

Yet even Bodin, the most exclusive and inflexible theorist of the environment, was aware that his model did not adequately explain some forms of change. He finally had to accept a certain degree of human responsibility: 'but anyone seeking to understand how diet, laws and customs have the power to change nature has only to look at the peoples of Germany who, in the time of Tacitus, had no religion, no science and no form of republic yet today cede nothing to other peoples in all these domains.' On the other hand, the Romans had 'lost all the splendours and virtues of their fathers'. These considerations seem enough to invalidate Bodin's entire system but he was a theorist who believed that exceptions simply confirm the rule.

A DIGRESSION ON THE AIR: ROBERT BURTON

The English scholar Robert Burton, author of *The Anatomy of Melancholy* (published in 1621 and in its sixth edition by 1660), was attracted by the same subject but approached it in a very different way from Bodin.[26] Burton devotes one section of his vast and erudite essay to a 'Digression on Ayr' and invites us to share his astonishment at the prodigious diversity of things. This is not a system but a kaleidoscope. Apparently, there are no rules (whereas Bodin found them everywhere). Why are human beings so different? What is responsible for the inexhaustible variety of temperaments, colours, plants, birds and animals? The air? The soil? The influence of the stars?

Whatever the case, Burton doubts that the congruence of climate and latitude is a convincing explanation. The Spanish and the

Italians belong to the white race: in the opposite hemisphere, and precisely on the same latitude, the inhabitants of the Cape of Good Hope are black. It is extremely cold in Moscow but in England and Ireland, again on the same latitude, the climate is mild and humid.

Burton believes the quality of the air is at the root of this confusing diversity and is particularly responsible for the 'explosion' of the human race: 'According to the state of the air, the inhabitants are dull, hearty, witty, subtle, neat, cleanly, clownish, sick and robust.' Egyptians, for example, are noted for their intelligence and merriment, the result, in all probability, of the pure air they breathe. As melancholy is the author's principal subject, this observation leads to practical advice: a frequent change of air is the best remedy for melancholy and all other ills that afflict mind and body.

These views are not entirely new. Hippocrates had included air in the title of his treatise; he had regarded it as one of the constitutive elements of 'climate'. But it had long been thought that the division of the inhabitable parts of the planet into 'zones' or 'climates' was sufficient as an organizing principle. To a great extent, the qualities or defects of the air depended on the climatic context. Whether hot, cold, dry or wet, the air is the medium through which the climate transmits its messages. But other elements could make a significant contribution to the composition of the atmosphere (topography, vegetation, emanations from the soil, etc.). Air was a subtler element than climate and more difficult to grasp. It may form different combinations within a particular climate; a further complication, but also a potential explanation for the infinite variety of things, a variety that climatic divisions could only partially justify. Wherever we are, we breathe the air specific to the locality and behave accordingly.

There had been long-standing agreement that human societies were fashioned by their natural environment.[27] Is this prejudice or truth? Ancient conventions left modern science with many questions to resolve. But does science have to come to terms with both tradition (the multitude of received ideas) and its own cultural and ideological context? We are about to observe how the Enlightenment, the era that subjected existing conceptions of the world to radical scrutiny, dealt with the problem.

TWO

The Climate of the Philosophers:
The Eighteenth Century

TOWARDS A SCIENCE OF SOCIETY: WHAT PLACE FOR THE CLIMATE?

The process of intellectual change that had begun in the West several centuries earlier accelerated during the eighteenth century, the age of Enlightenment and Reason, in which a God-centred world would give way to one based on science and rationality. The universe began to be seen as a vast, minutely regulated machine. The new way of looking at things was just as absolutist as the theological perspective, but Providence was yielding to 'scientific laws'. Newton, venerated like a god, symbolized the new science. Indeed, by formulating his law of universal attraction he had subjected the entire universe to a principle of order. Henceforth, for many philosophers, only 'physics' would count, a focus that extended to human society. Like the physical universe, the human universe was structured around rigorously defined relationships and functioned like a precision mechanism. The new agenda entailed a quest for 'scientific laws' that conformed to the Newtonian model of extreme clarity and efficiency and which could be applied to every domain, including society and history. But where, in the 'human sciences', was the great unifying principle, the equivalent of universal attraction in the physical world, to be found? To some thinkers, climate seemed perfectly suited to this purpose.

The scientific project of the Enlightenment was closely linked to its social and political ambitions. Society and government were to be restructured around laws and institutions that conformed to Reason and the general interest. This vast programme of reform would sometimes lead to revolutions, as in America and France. How was it related to climate? In an echo of Jean Bodin, if laws and institutions were to function properly, they had to be adapted to the character of each people, and the character of peoples was shaped by climate.

In many instances, the emerging general science of society accepted that climate had a determining role. But this approach had its opponents, who either simply refused to regard climate as a social and historical agent or saw it as of little importance. There was also a middle position: climate was deemed worthy of consideration but not accepted as decisive; it was forced to concede to the importance of human and social factors. Roles were already being reversed: Man was becoming the dynamic factor through his ability to modify climate and to alter existing natural balances as he pursued his own projects.

The eighteenth century had taken an evolutionist turn (which would bear fruit in the following century) and had begun to envisage the idea of progress, an extremely vague concept until that time. Scholars were attracted to climate because of its potential as a universal, unifying principle. But it was difficult to reconcile with evolution and still less with progress, and opinions differed. The science of society was proving more refractory than the movement of the planets. Moreover, it is important to remember that the eighteenth century was the heyday of philosophy. The philosopher's laboratory is his own mind.

Let us begin with the proponents of climate theory. After the somewhat empirical interpretations advanced by Hippocrates, Ibn Khaldun and Jean Bodin, the time had come for true science, a general science of society chiefly centred on climate. The fourth great classic of climate theory, *De l'Esprit des lois* by Charles de Secondat, Baron Montesquieu (1689–1755) was published in 1748. A whole team of travellers, authors and scholars had prepared the ground for Montesquieu. Travellers supplied the primary material in the form of descriptions of people and places. The Frenchman Jean Chardin (1643–1713), author of *Voyage en Perse et aux Indes orientales* (1686), had spent several years in Persia and claimed to have observed at first hand the destructive effects of heat on the human mind. That explained why Asian learning and achievement did not match that of Europe. Chardin passes quickly from descriptions to generalizations, considering climate chiefly responsible for the different dispositions and customs found in every country.

As for the theorists, the Abbé Jean-Baptiste Dubos (1670–1742) made a notable contribution with his *Réflexions critiques sur la poésie et la peinture* (1719). Poetry, painting and climate may seem an odd mixture but nothing was forbidden to seekers of first causes. Like Burton before him, Dubos gave prominence to the air, which seemed to explain a wide variety of phenomena, including poetry and painting. He began with an examination of national character, which always conformed to the qualities of the air and, specifically, of air temperature (whether hot or cold) and composition. Climatic diversity was responsible for the diversity of the human species, a range of differences that extended beyond the physical to the spiritual, intellectual and moral spheres. Like

Ibn Khaldun, Dubos believed that human beings change when they move from one climate to another: 'It has taken a mere ten centuries to render the descendants of the same father and mother as different as the Negroes and the Swedes are today.' He offers the example of the Portuguese who settled in Africa – after a few generations they were already beginning to resemble black peoples! The opposite also applied: 'We may believe that a colony of Negroes established in England would eventually lose the colour natural to Negroes.'[1] As for the link between climate and civilization, Dubos thought that cold and heat were harmful only when excessive: 'Far from restricting the temperature suited to the culture of sciences and fine arts to a range of four or five degrees of latitude, I believe that it can extend to twenty or twenty-five degrees.'[2] As Europe alone extended over more than 25°, this was not a very generous estimate.

When it came to historical evolution, Dubos had fewer scruples even than Bodin. Gradual changes in the condition and behaviour of peoples were bound to have some effect on the theory of climatic determinism. Bodin noted the difference between modern Germans and their Germanic ancestors. To Dubos the Germans of his day seemed identical to those observed by Tacitus. Similarly: 'Although the French are mainly descended from the Germans and other barbarians who settled in the Gallic lands, they have the same proclivities and the same mental characteristics as the ancient Gauls.'[3] (Leaving aside the implied ancestry, we should note that genetic inheritance is not a factor here; only local climates count. Whoever settles in Gaul, whatever his origin, becomes a Gaul or a Frenchman by virtue of the climate alone.)

However, it was difficult to deny a certain degree of historical evolution. Dubos put this down to 'emanations'. The air was continuously enriched by particles from the earth's crust (which was of a variable composition in space and time). We do not breathe

the same air from one year to the next, which explains both the changes that occur in a single country and the climatic oscillations observable over the course of time. Without this variation in the nature of the air, the climate would never change and history would stand still: 'The difference observable in the talents of the inhabitants of the same country over different centuries should be attributed to variations in the air in that country.'[4] Thus the system is complete and exclusive: the last word in climatic interpretation.

The Scots doctor and writer John Arbuthnot (1667–1735) made a significant contribution to establishing the climate–humanity relationship as a scientific equation with *An Essay Concerning the Effects of the Air on Human Bodies* (1733). Once again, the properties of the air were emphasized. Arbuthnot introduced a new element, atmospheric pressure, which could be measured and therefore lent credence to an otherwise experimental argument. In the northern hemisphere, he explained, the barometer was subject to considerable variations; consequently, the fibres of the human body were subjected to oscillatory movements. Cold acted as a stimulant. This corporeal dynamic influenced the soul and the passions and was expressed by greater energy and courage. As the barometer was more stable in hot climates, the 'fibres' behaved in a more uniform fashion, making more uniform the dispositions of the mind. The resulting character was lazy and indolent and marked by a 'disposition to slavery'.[5] Remarkably, Arbuthnot's 'scientific' method arrived at precisely the same conclusions as the doctrine propounded by Hippocrates (either because it reflected reality or because prejudice was more powerful than science!). The Greeks and Romans preferred the Mediterranean climate; the Scotsman came from colder climes and was proud of his own country. Early scholars had placed the British Isles at the limits of the known world and had peopled them with savages and cannibals, but to Arbuthnot, Britain represented the norm.

Arbuthnot's scientific investigations did not stop there. He studied the composition of the air, which, apart from its own properties, also benefited from the Earth's exhalations, an idea that Dubos had considered but had not developed. The atmosphere is constantly enriched by volcanic emanations and by salts and particles from the Earth's crust. Thus the air we breathe is a synthesis of all that surrounds us, a condition that justifies its influence over the human body and human behaviour.

Even language is affected by the air. The harsh speech of the peoples of the north was explained by their reluctance to open their mouths in the cold air, which resulted in an abundance of consonants. Conversely, inhabitants of hot countries opened their mouths wide, so their language was rich in vowels.[6] So simple and so perfect was science!

MONTESQUIEU: THE PRIMACY OF CLIMATE

And now we come to Montesquieu, Arbuthnot's immediate successor. Borrowing some of the Scotsman's ideas, Montesquieu also intended to proceed in a scientific and above all experimental manner. But how was he to experiment and measure the influence of climate on societies and civilizations with the required degree of precision? Nothing could be simpler – with the aid of a sheep's tongue. By freezing and then thawing this organ Montesquieu could observe the contraction and dilation of the taste buds. When the findings were applied to the human body, to individuals and ethnic groups, the experiment proved that,

Cold air constringes the extremities of the external fibres of the body; this increases their elasticity, and favours the return of the blood from the extreme parts of the heart. It contracts those very fibres; consequently it increases also their force. On the contrary, warm air relaxes and lengthens the extremes of the fibres; of course it diminishes their force and elasticity.

As for the physical and especially the moral consequences of these observations:

People are, therefore, more vigorous in cold climates. Here the action of the heart and the reaction of the extremities of the fibres are better performed, the temperature of the humors is greater, the blood moves more freely towards the heart, and reciprocally the heart has more power. This superiority of strength must produce various effects; for instance, a greater boldness, that is, more courage; a greater sense of superiority, that is, less desire for revenge; a greater opinion of security, that is, more frankness, less suspicion, policy and cunning.

On the other hand:

Put a man into a close, warm place, and for the reasons above given he will feel a great faintness. If under this circumstance you propose a bold enterprise to him, I believe you will find him very little disposed towards it; his present weakness will throw him into despondency; he will be afraid of everything, being in a state of total incapacity. The inhabitants of warm countries are, like old men, timorous; the people in cold countries are, like young men, brave.

Similarly:

In cold countries they have very little sensibility for pleasure; in temperate countries, they have more; in warm countries,

their sensibility is exquisite . . . In northern climates scarcely
has the animal part of love a power of making itself felt . . . In
warmer climates it is liked for its own sake, it is the only cause
of happiness, it is life itself.[7]

There are so many things to be learned from a sheep's tongue
(provided you ask it the right questions).

Montesquieu is less interested in the composition of the air than
some of his predecessors but he certainly believes that climate
offers an explanation for the social structures, manners and laws
that differ so much from one country to another. Slavery is unac-
ceptable in European countries but becomes understandable, if
not justified, among peoples living in hot climates; as they are idle
by nature, they have to be forced to work. Moreover, their lack of
energy and reaction reinforces the supremacy of the dominant
class and encourages despotic tendencies.[8] The blatant inequality
between the sexes in hot countries is also due to climate. Girls
ripen quickly, becoming nubile at eight or ten; at twenty they are
old and have lost their beauty, their principal weapon. This also
accounts for polygamy (the men periodically enlarge their families
with younger women), and explains why Islam flourishes in the
hot countries of Asia but cannot gain a foothold in Europe, where
a relative equality between the sexes exists thanks to the slower
ageing process in women, a benefit endowed by a cooler climate.[9]
And finally, it is no less apparent why women are isolated in these
hot societies, where heat has to be taken metaphorically as well as
literally; as they were just as sexually obsessed as the men it would
be dangerous to leave them alone together.[10]

The system accounts for everything. There is no real temperate
zone in Asia, Montesquieu tells us. The powerful races of the cold
north and the weaker races of the warm south live in close proximity to each other, a situation which provides the key to the

endless history of conquests in Asia: the North periodically invades the South.[11]

On the other hand, Montesquieu thinks Russia is almost European, essentially identical to the countries of the West. Indeed, the Russian climate is similar to that of western Europe, a fact that had guaranteed the success of Peter the Great's modernization programme. The Tsar had simply obeyed the dictates of the climate:

> What rendered the change the more easy was that their manners at that time were foreign to the climate, and had been introduced among them by conquest and by a mixture of nations. Peter the Great, in giving the manners and customs of Europe to a European nation, found a facility which he did not himself expect.

Some of the more authoritarian measures might have been avoided, for all Russia asked for was greater integration into the European community.[12] This was both a climatological and a political illusion. We can make a stronger case if we reverse the argument: Russia has a different climate; as a consequence the country is different and will remain so! After fine-tuning his climatic interpretation of Peter the Great's reign, the philosopher, highly satisfied with his demonstration, hit upon the fine formula: 'The empire of climate is the first, the most powerful, of all empires.'[13] But philosophers possess even greater power – they can remodel the world as they please.

Climatic virtues continued their northward drift in Montesquieu's work. Bodin's southerners, weaker and less energetic than the peoples of the North, had still had the monopoly on intelligence. By Montesquieu's time, however, the picture had changed. From now on, southerners were condemned to idleness and lovemaking – *la dolce vita*, in short. Meanwhile the North, the centre of thought and action, had commandeered the march of civilization.

We should be wary of oversimplifying Montesquieu's ideas. *De l'Esprit des lois* is a kind of encyclopaedia of the social sciences and omits nothing. The author accepts that many other factors besides climate – religion, laws, government, trade, historical traditions, customs etc. – exercise an influence over human communities. The law in particular is undeniably efficient: a legislator can determine a new course in the evolution of a people. We are therefore a long way from the tyranny of a single principle and the path of progress remains open. However, despite the interaction of various factors, a hierarchy still exists. Climate, by virtue of its power to define the limits of the possible and the impossible, remains the governing factor.

DAVID HUME VERSUS THE EMPIRE OF CLIMATE

Dr Arbuthnot had prepared the ground for Montesquieu, but another Scot, the philosopher David Hume (1711–1776), produced a systematic and remarkably confident refutation of the latter's work. Hume's *Of National Characters* advances nine arguments to demolish the theory that the constitution of national identities is determined by the 'empire' of climate and by nature in general.[14]

> 1. Hume begins with China, a country held in highly regard by the eighteenth-century Western intelligentsia: 'The Chinese have the greatest uniformity of character imaginable; though the air and climate, in different parts of those vast dominions, admit of very considerable variations.'

> 2. Conversely, small neighbouring countries sharing the same climate often present quite different profiles. 'Athens and

Thebes were but a short day's journey from each other; though the Athenians were as remarkable for ingenuity, politeness and gaiety, as the Thebans for dullness, rusticity, and a phlegmatic temper.'

3. 'The same national character commonly follows the authority of government to a precise boundary; and upon crossing a river or passing a mountain, one finds a new set of manners, with a new government.' The Spanish are very different to the southern French, although separated by nothing more than a frontier arbitrarily imposed after a succession of battles, negotiations and marriages.

4. Widely dispersed peoples like the Jews and Armenians preserve their particular characters, even when they settle in unfamiliar environments and live among very different peoples.

5. 'Where any accident, as a difference in language or religion, keeps two nations, inhabiting the same country, from mixing with each other, they will preserve, during several centuries, a distinct and even opposite set of manners. The integrity, gravity, and bravery of the Turks, form an exact contrast to the deceit, levity, and cowardice of the modern Greeks.' Hume is hostile to climatic interpretations but still susceptible to national prejudices: he seems to prefer the Turks to the Greeks – the age of Lord Byron had yet to arrive. But the argument itself is difficult to refute.

6. The Spanish, French, English and Dutch who leave home and settle in various parts of the world preserve their manners and other distinctive traits, even in the tropics (whereas Dubos had claimed their skin rapidly darkened).

7. People living in the same climate change over time. Moreover, this continuous process of cultural and social evolution within a relatively stable natural environment exposes the most vulnerable point in climatic theory: 'The ingenuity, industry, and activity of the ancient Greeks have nothing in common with the stupidity and indolence of the present inhabitants of those regions' (clearly, Hume did not appreciate the modern Greeks). As for the British: 'our ancestors, a few centuries ago, were sunk into the most abject superstition, last century they were inflamed with the most furious enthusiasm, and are now settled into the most cool indifference with regard to religious matters, that is to be found in any nation of the world.'

8. 'Where several neighbouring nations have a very close communication together, either by policy, commerce, or travelling, they acquire a similitude of manners, proportioned to the communication.'

9. 'We may often remark a wonderful mixture of manners and characters in the same nation, speaking the same language, and subject to the same government.' England provides a good example of a country in which liberal government and an open and differentiated society have engendered a great diversity of manners and mentalities. Given such diversity, Hume is reluctant to accept that the English could be defined in terms of a determined national character.

These speculations leave little room for climatic interpretation. Hume is prepared to accept (with reservations) that climate might have some influence in two domains: northerners' use of alcohol and southern sexuality. 'Wine and distilled spirits warm the frozen blood in the colder climates, and fortify men against the injuries of the weather: as the genial heat of the sun, in the countries exposed to his beams, inflames the blood, and exalts the passion between the sexes.' There are numerous exceptions to this 'rule', however: the ancient Greeks – men of the south – were fond of wine and preferred the company of men to that of women.

The whole schema hinged on two series of interpretations: those founded on *physical* causes (climate, air, the natural world), and those that gave primacy to *moral* causes. Hume claims that 'the nature of the government, the revolutions of public affairs, the plenty or penury in which the people live, the situation of the nation with regard to its neighbours, and such like circumstances' belong to the latter category. The term 'moral' therefore covers a broad range of political, social and moral causes. Although both *physical* and *moral* schools invoked a wide range of factors, the eighteenth-century mind had a tendency to simplify matters. Physical causes could not be reduced to climate but were manifestations of it. The many kinds of moral causes were chiefly related to governance, the way a country was led and administered. There were good and bad climates and good and bad governments. Taken separately or together, these two factors were primarily responsible for national character and history.

Hume correctly observes that every nation is an assembly of diverse components. A specific national character is therefore hard to identify and not much more than a strongly simplified and synthesized image (which did not stop the philosopher subscribing a little too eagerly to certain favourable or unfavourable national clichés; it is easier to construct a theory than to apply it). Each community exists in a state of continuous evolution and is sometimes affected by radical changes; there can be no static or definitive 'national character'. Hume's ideas are representative of the cosmopolitan spirit of the Enlightenment; they appeared just before the emergence of modern nationalist ideologies that imposed a clear and rigid image of national character (as well as the idea that each nation possessed its own 'soul', its own 'destiny'). Two hundred and fifty years later, as we are in the process of discarding the notion of a monolithic national identity, his arguments seem quite contemporary.

Nevertheless, Hume was just as exclusive as Montesquieu. The Frenchman had elevated climate to the rank of supreme principle; the Scotsman quite simply denied it. Yet climate is an undeniable presence. The determinism of the Enlightenment was somewhat lacking in subtlety and its mechanistic arguments linking causes to effects inevitably led to arbitrary choices.

PHYSICAL OR MORAL CAUSES?

Who was right, Montesquieu or Hume? Was it a matter of physical or of moral causes? A bitter philosophical battle broke out between supporters and critics of climate theory.

Very occasionally we come across an interpretation that lends equal weight to the two rival principles. Around 1820, the British traveller William Wilkinson was struck by the apathy he observed, particularly among the peasantry, in the Romanian territories of Wallachia and Moldavia. This condition could not be explained simply by servitude and oppression: climate also played a role. Climatic fluctuations and marshy ground were responsible for a certain 'dejection' that affected the flora and fauna as well. There was nothing better than a good government and a good climate and nothing worse than a bad government combined with a bad climate, a view that reconciled the arguments of Montesquieu and Hume.[15]

But we usually opt for one camp or another, or at least express a preference. The *Encyclopédie* adopted Montesquieu's point of view. In the third volume (1753), d'Alembert's article on climate entirely supported the author of *De l'Esprit des lois* and rejected any criticism of his system.[16]

Edward Gibbon (1737–1794) provided a detailed climatic interpretation in his *History of the Decline and Fall of the Roman Empire* (1776–88). He depicted the confrontation between Romans and Germans in climatic terms. Northern Europe was colder at that time according to available sources, although, given the amount of sunshine Greek and Latin authors enjoyed, they were sometimes tempted to exaggerate the rigours of the northern climate. Gibbon took account of possible distortions but believed the indications were sufficient to support the hypothesis. As a consequence, the robustness of the Germans, their courage, and their success in the bloody winter campaigns demoralized the Romans. On the other hand, when the same Germans settled in the south they lost their energy, which literally melted under the rays of the Mediterranean sun.[17]

Voltaire tended to take Hume's position. A specialist in the demolition of received ideas, this philosopher–polemicist found it easy to ridicule a thesis that presented so many weak points. The article 'Climat' in his *Dictionnaire philosophique* (a collection of essays from the series *Questions sur l'Encyclopédie*, published between 1770 and 1772) is a typically witty attack. It eschews Hume's systematic approach but advances arguments, particularly of a historical nature, similar to those of the Scottish philosopher. Chardin had boldly suggested that a hot climate was not conducive to intellectual activity. However, the Persian poet Sadi had not been adversely affected, nor Archimedes, the greatest scholar in antiquity, who came from Sicily, an even hotter place than Persia. Voltaire accepts that the Greeks and Romans had changed a great deal since antiquity (and not at all to their advantage) while the English had changed for the better:

Cicero made many joking references to the English in his letters. He asked his brother Quintus, Caesar's lieutenant, to let him know if he came across any great philosophers during the English expedition. He did not suspect that one day this country would produce mathematicians whom he would never have been able to understand. However, the climate has not changed and the sky over London is just as cloudy as it was then.[18]

The dominant factor is not climate but time: 'Bodies and minds change completely over time. Perhaps one day the Americans will come over and teach the arts to the peoples of Europe.' (It is tempting to say that Voltaire's prediction is being fulfilled but in fact he was thinking of native Americans rather than Americans of European stock.) Voltaire concluded that: 'Climate has some power, government one hundred times more and the combination of religion and government even more.'

The French philosopher Helvétius (1715–1771) also supported social and moral causes. According to De l'Esprit (1758), the fact that peoples evolve in very different ways owes more to education and the quality of government than to the natural world. There are no privileged nations; the arts and sciences have gradually taken root in almost every climate.[19]

Turgot (1727–1781), an economist and reforming statesman, approached the subject in Esquisse d'un plan pour la géographie politique, a work that never got beyond the planning stage. He believed that the use of climate to interpret differences between civilizations had no foundation and criticized 'the false way we have applied it to the characters of peoples and to their languages, to the vivacity of the imagination, the plurality of women and the servitude of Asians'. Montesquieu is the principal target here. Turgot stresses 'the necessity of exhausting moral causes before assuming the right to claim that climate has some physical influence'.[20]

The climate controversy played its part in one of the intellectual and ideological contradictions of the Enlightenment. On the one hand, the West was increasingly proud of its superiority, a condition that encouraged racism. On the other, it was marked by a universalist spirit that denied any essential superiority; many philosophers admired China and some spoke favourably of the native Americans or the Polynesians. Yet Africa and the black race were systematically devalued. The systematic mentality of the Enlightenment placed the black person halfway between white man and monkey.[21]

The concept of race introduced further complications to the range of interpretations. Racism was one of the Enlightenment's many philosophical and scientific innovations. In fact, like so many of the emblematic representations that were revised in the light of the new spirit of philosophy, racial prejudice had a long history. But the eighteenth century invested it with doctrinal rigour and armed it with scientific credibility. The famous system of natural classification devised by Swedish naturalist Carl von Linné (1707–1778)[22] organized things in the Cartesian manner so dear to the era: there were four continents (Australia was not yet known) and four human races (European, Asian, American and African), each of which had its own colour, temperament and degree of civilization. Europeans were at the top, Africans at the bottom and Asians in between. Nuances no longer counted: the Asian was yellow, the African black and the European white (or more precisely blonde and blue-eyed, as the Swede Carl von Linné saw it). The next revelation, made by the Dutch anatomist Peter Camper (1722–1789), concerned the *facial angle*, the result of an intersection of two cranial lines, one drawn between the tip of the nose and the opening of the ear, the other between the projection of the forehead and the most prominent part of the jaw. The facial angle served as a measure of intelligence (skull formation indicated brain development). The superior intelligence of the European was finally and scientifically established: his facial angle ranged from 80 degrees to a maximum of 90 degrees. The 'yellow races' had an angle of about 75 degrees, while the Negro's was no more than 70 (compared to 58 for an orang-utan).

The pre-eminence of the European climate (especially its Nordic version) and the white race (also preferably in its northern version), went hand in hand. But was there a relationship of cause and effect? Perplexity reigned on this point. It did indeed seem that sun and heat were partly responsible for the divergence in humanity that black peoples (subjected to the overwhelming tropical sun) and whites (living in a cooler, less sunny climate) represented. This could provide an explanation for colour and temperament. But the races had other morphological characteristics not so easily explained in terms of climate.

The debate remained unresolved. We have seen how Dubos believed that racial distinctions were rapidly shaped by climate. Most biologists accepted the idea of an original and unique race (an interpretation that agreed with the Bible). Von Linné thought so, as did the German naturalist J. F. Blumenbach (1752–1840), who also believed that human differences were the result of the combined action of climate, food and culture.[23] According to the French naturalist Buffon (1707–1788), 'white appears to be the primitive colour of nature and is altered and changed by climate, food and manners'.[24] 'Other' races were nothing more than degenerate whites! Climate usually took pride of place when the causes of this separation were discussed.

But the 'monogenists', supporters of the view that humanity descended from a single ancestor, had to contend with the 'polygenists' who thought that separate races or different human 'species' had existed from the beginning. They had been created either by God or by Nature, probably so that they could more successfully adapt to different natural environments and climates. However, their existence owed nothing to climatic influences. Henry Home, Lord Kames, a Scots philosopher, addressed the matter in a book entitled *Sketches of the History of Man* (1778). He criticized Buffon's 'evolutionism' and offered a long series of examples from nature to prove that there was no relation between race and climate. Abyssinians are different from other black peoples although they live under the same climate. 'Yellow' races are to be found in both polar regions and torrid zones. Norwegians and Finns bear little resemblance to Lapps although all three live in proximity to each other. Home was firmly convinced that: 'neither temper nor talents have much dependence on climate'.[25]

Enlightenment thinkers were thus confronted with differing interpretations. Race was either strictly determined by the physical environment (particularly climate) or influenced by it in a more subtle and varied way. Another theory advocated the total separation of the two concepts, giving race an 'independent' status. Whatever the case, race and environment, even when separated, achieved a kind of symbiotic relationship. Their ideological function, at a time of Western expansion, was to provide irrefutable scientific arguments to support the claim of Western supremacy.

HERDER: CLIMATE AND PEOPLES, ACTION AND REACTION

Most eighteenth-century scholars and philosophers preferred clear-cut solutions. They tended either to accord climate prime position or simply ignore it. However, some attempts were made to find a balance between the physical world and moral and social causal factors. The thinkers who followed this path often had difficulty in assessing the true importance of each factor; they often wavered between an adherence to a certain geographic and climatic determinism and the advancement of socially based arguments.

This hesitation is apparent in the work of Johann Gottfried Herder (1744–1803), author of *Ideen zur Philosophie der Geschichte der Menschheit* (1784–91), one of the period's most ambitious and influential treatises on the philosophy of history. Some passages are strictly determinist in the tradition of Montesquieu. According to Herder, the pattern for human history had been designed by nature; mountains, rivers and seas impose spatial restrictions; different topographies produce different histories. Each human community bears the mark of its environment: 'the difference that exists between men, as well as between all the other productions of the terrestrial sphere, must be measured by the specific difference of the environment in which we live.'[26]

The zone that generates civilizations is characterized by a temperate climate. Europe (particularly the Mediterranean area) and a part of Asia are suitable because:

> Man does not have to endure the piercing cold of the Samoyeds, nor the burning, salt-laden winds of the Mongol. Nor, on the other hand, is he exposed to the consuming heat of the African deserts and sands; nor to the humidity or rapid changes of the American climate; there are no enormous mountains as on the equator, or frozen peaks as in the polar regions.[27]

But Herder also believes in the 'spirit of peoples', an ensemble of inherited biological and physical characteristics that, though initially fashioned by the environment, retain a high degree of autonomy. Black peoples do not turn white when they move from one climate to another, as Dubos believed. Besides, man also has an effect on climate; he can significantly modify its original characteristics. He is subjected to the effects of a climate that he had himself created. For example, the European forests had given way to agriculture while the Egyptians had gained control over the waters of the Nile. Man is 'placed like a Lord of the Earth'; he has the ability to modify the effects of nature's agency. All in all, it is a case of human-climatic interference rather than of unilateral climatic tyranny. Herder is reluctant to pronounce on the effects of climate and contradicts some of his earlier statements by claiming that it does not impose a regime but merely stimulates tendencies; it adds a brush stroke, nothing more, to the overall picture of life.[28]

Where does that leave us? Rather lost in the maze of interpretations. Is climate sovereign, secondary to other factors or shaped by man? A difficult problem. ˙

ROBERTSON AND THE AMERICAN LABORATORY

If scientists wished to conduct experiments into the relationship between climate and society, there were better ways than freezing and thawing a sheep's tongue or philosophizing as one strolled in one's garden. They had an immense laboratory at their disposal: America. America offered great geographical and climatic diversity as well as a mosaic of populations that were either 'primitive' or situated on the first rungs of civilization's ladder. They could be studied in relation to their habitat, while the recent wave of European colonization might afford insights into the problem of adapting to a significantly different environment.

The best synthesis of this ensemble of problems was made by Scotsman William Robertson (1721–1793), one of the most celebrated historians of his day. His *History of America* (1777), presents a significantly more complex, nuanced and balanced picture than the considerations of the philosophers we have consulted. Less preoccupied with discovering absolute principles, he appears more open to the diversity of things and the interaction of different phenomena.

Robertson begins with a meticulous examination of America's geography and natural environment, a project that integrates historical development into his physical framework. There is an element of geographical determinism but it is limited in space and time. He believes that climate is the dominant force in extreme zones and influences primitive populations. These reasons – climatic and human – are enough to justify his assertion that Africa is condemned to a 'diminished' existence. On the other hand, he claims that civilized societies, through their inventions and industry, are eventually able to remedy most of the flaws and inconveniences to be found in all temperatures.

Nature offers more or less good conditions but man can either submit to them or take appropriate action. Robertson's thoughts on the domestication of animals are highly significant in this respect. The native Americans were greatly handicapped by the absence of domestic animals. This was only partly nature's fault. Species susceptible to domestication were less numerous in America than in the Old World, but they did exist, the bison, a cousin of the ox, being one example. The fact was that man did not domesticate certain animals that could have been domesticated. This was his own responsibility, not that of nature or climate.

Robertson was not about to embrace the scepticism of Hume and deny the existence of climate. But the 'law of climate' contains too many exceptions and cannot be regarded as efficient: the character and actions of peoples cannot be explained by a single cause. There seems to be a stronger case for moral and political causes.

Yet natural conditions are modified by man. 'By casting an eye over the face of the inhabited globe, we see that much of the beauty and fertility that we attribute to the hand of nature is the work of Man. These efforts, when they are pursued over the course of centuries, perfect the qualities of the soil and even change its appearance.'[29] Uncultivated land allows climate to do its worst and also corrupts the air; it is the source of all manner of illnesses. Once man has tamed the American environment, it will offer him much more favourable conditions.

REGULATING THE TEMPERATURE: *the first steps*

Both Herder and Robertson believed that human activity had an impact on climate and environment. Such views triggered the great paradigm shift that occurred in the eighteenth century. Man was gradually breaking away from the 'empire' of climate and proposed to subject it to his will. His mission was to transform the surrounding environment according to his needs. The idea was not entirely new; Strabo had discussed it, for even in his day, it had seemed obvious that man had a direct influence on nature. However, during the Enlightenment and the following centuries the idea gained ground that, apart from his ability to cultivate land, he could also intervene in nature in such a radical way that he could recreate it to his own advantage. Once the process had begun, there was no stopping it. Ecological factors were ignored; sovereign Reason would have the same radical and benign effect on the natural world as it had had on society. The turning point came during the latter half of the eighteenth century, which symbolized the acceleration of growth and the crystallization of the modern idea of progress. These were the first steps on the road that would lead to technological civilization.

For Gibbon, the improvement in the European climate since the Classical age could be explained by deforestation and the expansion of agriculture. Social and economic progress brought about climatic progress:

The modern improvements sufficiently explain the causes of the diminution of the cold. These immense woods have been gradually cleared, which intercepted from the earth the rays of the sun. The morasses have been drained, and, in proportion as the soil has been cultivated, the air has become more temperate. Canada, at this day, is an exact picture of ancient Germany. Although situated in the same parallel with the finest provinces of France and England, that country experiences the most rigorous cold. The reindeer are very numerous, the ground is covered with deep and lasting snow, and the great river of St Lawrence is regularly frozen, in a season when the waters of the Seine and the Thames are usually free from ice.[30]

Gibbon would have been very disappointed to learn that the mildness of the northwest European climate owed a lot more to the warm waters of the Gulf Stream than to the progress of the European economy!

Buffon's *Epoques de la nature* (1778) contains some astonishing remarks. He too accepted that the nature had influenced the genesis of the early civilizations. But at a certain point in the evolutionary process, the relationship goes into reverse. Man becomes more powerful than nature and establishes his dominance over the planet:

Through his intelligence, animals have been tamed, subjugated, domesticated, reduced to eternal obedience; through his works, swamps have been drained, rivers contained, their cataracts effaced, the forests cleared, moorland cultivated . . . in short, the entire face of the Earth today bears the imprint of Man's power.[31]

Buffon observes that nature under cultivation is very different from nature in the raw. The France and Germany of his own day had changed dramatically since the Greco-Roman era; their climates had been modified by man, who had cut down the forests, drained the marshes and straightened the course of the rivers.

The more a population increases, the more the temperature rises, thanks to the heat given off by all living organisms, human and animal. This process is accelerated by human industry, especially the use of fire. The reduction of vegetation (which produces 'cold humidity') is another contributory factor. The temperature in great cities like Paris was already two or three degrees higher than those recorded in neighbouring regions. These observations lead to a revolutionary conclusion: climate could be regulated. For example: 'The addition or removal of a single forest in a country is sufficient to change its temperature.' It follows that: 'Man can modify the influences of the climate he lives under and fix, so to speak, its temperature to the point that suits him.' However, it would be 'more difficult to cool the Earth than to heat it'. This may seem like a premonition of global warming, but it was welcome news to the people of eighteenth-century Europe, who much preferred the warmth to the cold.

The distance between Montesquieu and Buffon is evident: the belief that man and society are shaped by climate has given way to a conviction that man has the power to modify and master it. The subjugation of climate to the human will is inscribed in a more general context: the affirmation of human potential. Man aimed to free himself from every constraint, including those imposed by God and Nature, and take control of his own destiny. A new era, rich in promise and danger, had begun.

THREE

The North at the Zenith

SCIENTISM, IMPERIALISM AND NATIONALISM

The eighteenth century had been the age of philosophy but the nineteenth century was to become the age of science. Its impressive scientific and technological achievements constitute the foundations of our own technological civilization. In the circumstances, we might have expected it to display a deeper, more nuanced understanding of human and social phenomena and of a theory of climate that, despite adaptations and refinements, was still derived from scholars who had died long before the birth of modern geography.

Yet for several reasons linked to historical and ideological conditions as well as to contemporary scientific attitudes, the theory still commanded respect. Science was advancing but, if the eighteenth century had represented the infancy of modern science, the nineteenth century typified its exuberant and impetuous youth. It was the era of scientism; science became a kind of religion expected to provide instant explanations for everything. In such a context, its arguments followed on from each other rather too easily, linking cause to effect in a summary and deterministic spirit. Theories were forged from 'causes' and 'effects' that required further elucidation. There seemed no need to abandon climatic theory; it was just a matter of consolidating its scientific framework.

The problem was compounded by the prestige enjoyed by the natural sciences. The speed of their advance in comparison with history, not to mention other burgeoning human sciences like sociology, resulted in a kind of hotchpotch of ideas. The notion gained ground that not only could the human environment be detached from the natural environment, but the 'laws' governing society and history might essentially be the same as those that governed nature. At this stage, it is worth pointing out that the evolutionist theory initially outlined by Lamarck and then perfected and firmly established by Darwin in *Evolution of the Species* (1859) had a considerable impact on the human sciences. In the absence of a proper system of laws, it was tempting to draw inspiration from the principles and rules of natural evolution.

Critics of a science of society that relied too heavily on climate, nature and biological laws soon came up with their own equally inflexible and reductionist systems. Marx believed in the dominance of the socio-economic network and had no time for climate. His argument was certainly more modern but, in keeping with the spirit of the times, it was still deterministic and simplistic.

Two concurrent historical developments left their indelible mark on nineteenth-century science. The first was western expansion. The West became the undisputed master of the planet, an achievement that succeeded in undermining every 'other' form of civilization. China, which had attracted the respect of eighteenth-century philosophers, was dismissed as 'an imbecilic and barbaric government' by Alexis de Tocqueville (1805–1859).[1] If the Chinese had sunk so low, imagine the position occupied by other races, particularly the black peoples, who had long been condemned to the bottom rung of the human ladder. The nineteenth century was racist, even more so than the preceding era, because the arrogance of the 'white man' had already reached a peak and because racial classification, increasingly refined through the multiplication of races and sub-races, benefited from an accumulation of 'scientific' arguments.[2]

Racism both reinforced and weakened climate theory. There was plenty of evidence to suggest that climate was responsible for racial distinctions. But, even if races were originally shaped by climate, they had a tendency to become autonomous entities. Some eighteenth-century philosophers and scholars had believed that a change in climatic conditions, or conditions of life in general, plus a good education, were likely to efface biological distinctions over a relatively short period of time. Nineteenth-century science was more reticent and distinctly more conservative on this point. The races were regarded as fixed entities; if there were indeed any possibility of transformation, it would be a slow and difficult process. Moreover, the dispute between 'monogenists' and 'poly-genists' continued unabated, although both focused on the origins of humanity rather than its present state. In fact both camps were tempted to emphasize racial distinctions. When imagined in this way, race takes precedence over climate. Black peoples were inferior not because it was so hot in Africa but simply because they were black!

Nationalist ideology – imperialism beyond the borders of Europe but nationalism within them – also exercised a major influence on the nineteenth century. The same mindset that had divided the world along racial lines went on to divide it into nations and later nation-states. The distinctions between a Frenchman, a German and an Englishman were obviously less pronounced than those between whites and blacks, but they were still thought extremely significant. This focus on human diversity gave rise to a new science: the psychology of peoples.[3] After the cosmopolitanism of the Enlightenment, Europe changed course and began to refine its divisions with great enthusiasm. While it was plain that many factors contributed to the formation of national characteristics, climate, and quite often race, were still advanced as primary agents. (Like Europe, the white race itself had fragmented; it had been seen as a single entity in the eighteenth century but by 1900 an anthropologist had counted no less than six European races and four 'sub-races', a total of ten 'biological' divisions in the European continent alone).[4]

Why, for example, are the Irish so different from the English? George Bernard Shaw provides one possible answer in the long 'theoretical' preface to his play *John Bull's Other Island* (1904). Shaw claims that there is no specifically Irish race distinct from the English 'race'. Economic conditions have something to do with it but the determining factor is climate. An Irish climate 'stamps an immigrant more deeply and durably in two years, apparently, than the English climate will in two hundred'.[5] It seemed that Irishness was a rapidly acquired yet permanent condition.

THE PERILS OF AFRICA

A wealth of seminal nineteenth-century texts helps us to understand this process of simplification and generalization. Karl Ritter (1779–1859), one of the founders of modern geography, specialized in the study of the relation between physical and human phenomena. His *Die Erdkunde im Verhältnis zur Natur und Geschichte des Menschen* (1817–18) is a classic of its kind, especially noteworthy for its profiles of the three continents of the Old World, although these are depicted with scant concern for nuance. Ritter suggests that the high historical destiny of Europe is inscribed in the very topography of the continent. Asia seems to be the antithesis of Europe. Africa is a uniform, almost undifferentiated mass, whose uniformity encompasses the vegetal and animal worlds and impedes human development, as it offers no stimulus for intelligence or civilization!

The real Africa is overwhelmed by an imaginary Africa that seems to soak up every prejudice particular to the white race. It is a torrid, dark, savage and dangerous continent. The white traveller is ill-advised to venture there, for he might never return. If not laid low by an inhospitable climate or exhausted by exotic fevers, he risks being devoured by wild beasts or cannibal tribes. It is hard to explain the long-delayed exploration of the African interior other than by a reticence that bordered on fear. The continent closest to Europe was the last to reveal its secrets.

Even by 1800, Europeans knew little of the Dark Continent apart from the outline of its coasts. James Bruce (1730–1794), a Scots explorer who had travelled in Abyssinia and had earned respect as an authority on African problems, went so far as to claim that that the peoples of Africa, even those living below the equator, did not belong to the same race as the Negroes. Inevitably, climate was responsible. Buffon took credit for this curious revelation:

> The entire centre of Africa is temperate and rather rainy; it is situated well above sea level and most of it is populated by people who are white or swarthy rather than black . . . The entire Negro race is much less in evidence here: I doubt it constitutes a hundredth part of humanity, since we are now informed that the African interior is populated by white men.[6]

The logic of high altitude, temperate climate and white skin is simply a curious strategy for normalizing an unknown continent in climatic and human terms. This 'whitewash' did not attract many disciples, however. Most Europeans persisted in their belief that Africa was hot, black and savage.

By the 1850s the West could no longer tolerate the blank spaces on its maps. Feeling strong enough to plant its flags in every part of the world, it began its assault on Africa. Burton and Speke led the quest for the sources of the Nile and Livingstone and Stanley mounted their expeditions into the interior. Jules Verne, however, opted for an 'aerial' crossing in his *Cinq semaines en ballon* (1863), a novel that reflects the extent of Western knowledge of Africa as well as attitudes towards it. Verne feared that an overland journey would entail too many risks: 'it is impossible to fight against the elements; against hunger, thirst and fever; against ferocious animals and even more ferocious tribes!'[7]

Yet Europeans gradually became accustomed to Africa and some even acquired a taste for the continent. Perhaps the African climate was not so bad as it had been portrayed.

SOCIETY BEFORE ENVIRONMENT

Proponents and critics of climatic causes continued to argue their case. Charles Comte (1782–1837), author of the massive *Traité de législation, ou exposition des lois générales suivant lesquelles les peuples prospèrent, dépérissent ou restent stationnaires* (1826–7), remarked: 'There are still many, even among the educated classes, who believe that the institutions and manners of other peoples are the product of the climate they live in: this opinion has become a kind of popular prejudice.' Apparently, it was all Montesquieu's fault. Comte's choice of title is revealing: it indicates his conviction that his compatriot's outline for a science of society needed to be redrawn on a different basis. Comte adopts an 'anti-climatic' position. He believes that, far from impeding historical development, the tropical climate had fostered the emergence of a series of major civilizations. On the other hand, there are discernable differences between peoples living in similar environments and similarities between peoples living in different environments. He suggests expanding the concept of 'environment' in order to get away from the obsession with climate and to incorporate a variety of elements including natural resources, the properties of the soil and the type and direction of watercourses. He also stresses the physical interdependence of society and environment. Environment is important but it should be considered in all its complexity and seen in relation to human and social factors.[8]

Alexis de Tocqueville deserves another mention at this point, for he is one of the few nineteenth-century political historians and commentators whose reputation continues to grow. Tocqueville begins *De la Démocratie en Amérique* (1835–40), his classic analysis of the American phenomenon, with a description of the country's geography that takes little account of physical interpretations. In fact, the new and untamed natural environment encountered by the first European settlers might have been been an essential factor in the crystallization of a specific mentality. However, this interpretation is contradicted by the fact that vast spaces and abundant natural resources are also to be found in South America, where history has taken a very different turn. Therefore: 'physical causes have less influence on the destiny of nations than we believe.' Laws are stronger than the natural environment and manners have even more weight than laws.[9] (But does the primacy of manners represent the last word in historical interpretation? How can their diversity be explained? Montesquieu had the answer – by climate!).

The nineteenth century maintained the impetus created in the preceding century. It had much more (although still insufficient) information at its disposal and seemed determined to resolve the social and historical equation, by devising a complete and perfect science that could either encompass a theory of climate or dispense with it altogether. Marx found no place for it his system of socioeconomic structures and laws. Auguste Comte, founder of positivism, incorporated it into his own project, believing that history and sociology could only benefit from the laws of nature, a belief strengthened by the impact of Darwin's work and the growing prestige of the natural sciences.

POTATOES AND VOLCANOES: *Buckle's system*

At this point an exceptional historian, Henry Thomas Buckle (1821–1862), author of the unfinished *History of Civilization in England* (1857–61), arrived on the scene. Buckle conceded that historians had worked hard and amassed a great deal of information. Unfortunately, their intelligence had rather let them down. None had come close to rivalling Newton's intellectual brilliance. Newtonian science was still the benchmark. (Though Newton himself had a rather simplistic view of history and his efforts in this field had not matched the splendour of his discoveries concerning the physical world. History, however, is very different from the movement of the planets and incomparably more complicated!)

Buckle set to work in the hope of becoming the Newton of history (or at least of blazing a trail for another Newton), making use of many other disciplines ranging from political economy to biology. He also aimed to take advantage of a brand new tool, statistics, and combine it with probability theory, a domain whose foundations had just been established by the Belgian mathematician Adolphe Quételet (1796–1874). With the aid of statistics, social data could finally be measured and integrated into series. The collective took precedence over the individual. Records indicated that almost the same number of suicides occurred each year. Similarly, the annual number of unaddressed letters remained constant. Therefore, beyond individual motivations, there was a consistency at the social level that made the formulation of laws possible and necessary. When approached in this way, history acquired as much credibility as the natural sciences.

Buckle believes that historical development is influenced by two general conditions: the physical and the mental. The former is divided into four categories: climate, food, soil and the general aspect of nature. Everything begins with the accumulation of wealth. Essentially, all the great Eastern civilizations – China, Egypt, India and Mesopotamia – had achieved this thanks to the fertility of the soil. Europe, on the other hand, is dominated by its climate. The fundamental differences between the two worlds had gradually increased over the centuries. The fertile soil that had allowed Asian civilizations to flourish had done little to stimulate human energy, which explains both their early rise and their stagnation: they had occupied a relatively unchanging world. European civilization, however, initially governed by climate and having less brilliant beginnings, had stimulated energy and initiative, proving a capacity for development unknown to civilizations content to reap the benefits of the soil.

Moreover, the lower temperatures affecting the northern part of Europe mean that its populations require more food, and substantially more meat. The inhabitants of southern regions consume less food and live chiefly on vegetables. This leads to markedly different demographic tendencies: limited population growth in cold countries (where food is scarcer and a greater quantity is needed to ensure survival) and conversely, a high birth rate in hot countries. The standard of living is therefore significantly higher in the north. Cold weather is also responsible for the greater social equality apparent in the north. The south, by contrast, is marked by social disparities characterized by the existence of small elites and impoverished masses (the conclusion was similar to Montesquieu's but supported by a battery of scientific arguments). Paradoxical as it may seem, a cheap and abundant supply of food inevitably leads to poverty. The theory could be manipulated to explain anomalies like Ireland. Why had the Irish, a northern race, been reduced to poverty? (Famine was rife in Ireland at the time, and the great wave of emigration had already begun.) Obviously, Buckle explained, because they live on potatoes, a crop with a very high yield. Overproduction had stimulated population growth, which in turn had led to poverty: there were simply too many mouths to feed.

So the history of the world is divided into two parts: non-European civilizations determined by the soil and European civilization shaped by climate. The production of wealth has gradually enabled Europe to free itself almost completely from the burden of the environment. There is a threshold beyond which history ceases to be governed by the power of nature and submits to the power of the human mind. Science and technology have triumphed to the extent that Europe is now capable of imposing its will on nature. But it had all started with climate.[10]

It is also interesting to note Buckle's emphasis on the broader effects of nature. In addition to the heat, the inhabitants of southern countries are almost 'crushed' by a nature so vast that it inspires fear and respect. This explains their fearful and superstitious character, very different to the rationality displayed by northern peoples. His thoughts on Europe, particularly Italy and Spain, are equally enlightening. Although neither country had contributed much to science, they had produced all the great painters and nearly all the great sculptors of the modern period. This could be explained by volcanic eruptions and earthquakes, phenomena that stimulated the senses and galvanized the imagination. Europe is therefore more rational and less imaginative than the other continents. But among Europeans, the English, untroubled by volcanic upheavals, are more rational than the Italians. Nature had allowed them to develop their intelligence undisturbed.

Curiously, Buckle had forgotten the role of the Netherlands in the history of art; for centuries it had been second only to Italy as a centre of artistic creation. Italy itself had made an enormous contribution to the genesis of modern science. However, there seemed to be no place for Rembrandt and Galileo in the new world order.

TAINE: *grass and beer*

It was left to Hippolyte Taine (1828–1893), French philosopher, historian and critic of literature and art, to explain how a country could produce great artists even when it lacked volcanoes. Taine, like Buckle, is a system-builder in the best (or worst) nineteenth-century tradition, believing that everything can be accounted for by the combined effects of race, environment and historical moment. He begins his analysis of Flemish art with some remarks on the Low Countries:

> We might say that in this country water creates grass, which creates cattle, which creates cheese, butter and meat which, when they are all combined with beer, create the inhabitant. Indeed, we can see the birth of the Flemish temperament in this rich existence and a physical environment saturated by moist air.[11]

This is a long chain of associations but the primary factor, air humidity, is climatic. The interpretation is all the more remarkable given that Taine was proposing to explain artistic production rather than cattle farming.

The same logic applies to Greece. Greek civilization has been shaped by landscape and climate:

> Nothing in this country is enormous or gigantic; external objects have no disproportionate or overwhelming dimensions . . . Everything is average, moderate, easily and clearly

perceptible to the senses . . . In this way, nature, through the forms with which it populates the mind, directly inclines the Greek towards fixed and clear-cut conceptions.[12]

Unlike Hume, Taine makes no unfavourable distinction between ancient and modern Greece.

RATZEL: *the tyranny of the environment*

Nineteenth-century science was fascinated by the relation between the natural world and human society. Everything seemed to encourage further investigation: the intrusion of the 'white man' into every corner of the globe; the growing interest in non-European civilizations and 'primitive' cultures situated, of course, in their natural context; the prevailing evolutionism and the tendency to explain the functioning of societies in biological terms. 'Ecology', a new discipline founded by the German biologist Ernst Haeckel (1834–1919) began to take its first steps and seemed destined for a brilliant career. It was entirely legitimate to subject the multitude of connections between all the constitutive elements of the universe to microscopic examination. But the nineteenth-century mind had difficulty in conceiving the world as an extremely complex and subtle network of interdependences. Even those who seemed to accept the existence of 'interference' simply split the argument into two equally rigid categories: nature's effect on man or man's effect on nature. The era was resolutely determinist and preferred simple relations of cause and effect. Even if the existence of several factors was acknowledged, one factor had to take precedence over the others, an original and determining principle.

Elisée Reclus (1830–1905), author of an immense geographical overview entitled *Nouvelle géographie universelle* (19 volumes, 1875–94), and the more theoretical *L'Homme et la terre* (6 volumes,

1905), thought that the constituents of each climatic zone, of soil and landscape, engendered distinct human and societal types; thus there were civilizations specific to deserts, mountains, steppes, forests, etc. Reclus introduces his universal geography with the claim that Russia should be excluded from the 'true Europe' on the grounds that it is: 'half Asian because of its extreme climate, monotonous country and interminable steppes'.[13] This is a very different opinion from the one expressed by his compatriot Montesquieu. It is interesting that Russia's exclusion is based solely on climate and physical geography; there is no reference to society or civilization. Apparently, Reclus considered it a foregone conclusion that a non-European climate and landscape could only produce a non-European civilization.

The Marquis de Custine (1790–1857) had defined attitudes to the Tsarist empire some years earlier in his famous *La Russie en 1839*: far from being European, the Russians are 'Chinese in disguise'. Nor, despite their claims, does their climate bear any similarity to the European model (once again climate and civilization go together):

> Among other boasts, I have heard many Russians claim that
> their climate is getting milder. Is it possible that God is
> complicit in the ambitions of these greedy people? Is it
> possible that He will endow them with the skies and the
> airs of the Midi? Are we about to see Athens in Lapland,
> Rome in Moscow and the riches of the Thames in the Gulf
> of Finland?[14]

The man who did most to refine the connections between geographical factors and human communities was the German geographer Friedrich Ratzel (1844–1904), one of the founders of human geography or, to use his own term, *anthropo-geography*. His principal work, entitled *Anthropoiegeographie*, appeared between

1882 and 1891. Ratzel started from a well-informed and rigorous basis. His initial training as a naturalist enabled him to broaden the scope of the enquiry, but also accounted for his tendency to view everything from a biological perspective. His systematic study of the relations between society and environment acknowledged man's impact on nature but was nonetheless conducted within the confines of a rather narrow determinism.

Climate is still the governing factor in Ratzel's work, either directly, through its effects on the human body, or indirectly, through the way it influences animal and plant life and the composition of the soil. The most favourable climate is obviously temperate and, no less obviously, the most successful regions are a little cooler. This has interesting consequences, even within established nations. Ratzel believed that the French, Italians, Germans and Americans of the northern USA were superior to their southern compatriots (but remained silent about a probable Scots superiority over the English). To a certain extent, the theory mirrors historical developments: Germany had just been unified by Prussia and Italy by Piedmont, while the North had recently defeated the South in the American Civil War. As for France, it had long been revolving around Paris. Ratzel himself came from southern Germany and was honest enough to admit his own inferiority. He was also preoccupied by the behaviour of populations descended from European stock settled in different, less favourable climates. The problem was of scientific interest but also had its practical side at a time of colonial expansion. The German geographer felt that an unfavourable climate was likely to have a detrimental effect on the colonists' physical and mental condition (moreover, the degree of adaptability differed from one people to another).[15]

Ellen C. Semple, an American admirer of Ratzel's work, developed and popularized his ideas in *American History and its Geographic Conditions* (1903) and *Influences of Geographic Environment, on the Basis of Ratzel's System of Anthropo-geography* (1911). Like Ratzel, Semple is aware of interdependences: the same natural conditions have different effects as societies develop over time; different parts of the world establish increasingly closer relationships that extend beyond climatic frontiers, etc. But Semple, like her master, often falls back on an almost tyrannical geographical determinism. This accounts for her descriptions of civilizations and ethnic mentalities that owe everything to the physical world: islands, steppes, deserts, mountains, etc., produce specific human groups. This is clear from her comments on mountain peoples:

> With this conservatism of the mountaineer is generally coupled suspicion toward strangers, extreme sensitiveness to criticism, superstition, strong religious feeling, and an intense love of home and family. The bitter struggle for existence makes him industrious, frugal, provident; and, when the marauding stage has been outgrown, he is peculiarly honest as a rule. Statistics of crime in mountain regions show few crimes against property though many against the person. When the mountain-bred man comes down into the plains, he brings with him therefore certain qualities which make him a formidable competitor in the struggle for existence – the strong muscles, unjaded nerves, iron purpose, and indifference to luxury bred in him by the hard conditions of his native environment.[16]

As for climate in the proper sense of the word, Semple, like Ratzel, regards the south with a certain scorn and, in accordance with climatic data, notes distinctions within the same racial groups.

> The northern peoples of Europe are energetic, provident, serious, thoughtful rather than emotional, cautious rather

than impulsive. The southerners of the sub-tropical Mediterranean basin are easy-going, improvident except under pressing necessity, gay, emotional, imaginative, all qualities which among the Negroes of the equatorial belt degenerate into grave racial faults. If, as many ethnologists maintain, the blonde Teutons of the north are a bleached out branch of the brunette Mediterranean race, this contrast in temperament is due to climate.[17]

The Scots differ from the English: 'The conditions which have differentiated Scotch from English have been climate, relief, location, geologic composition of the soil, and ethnic composition of the two peoples.' Semple made no mention of historical circumstances and gave no consideration to religious, cultural or social developments. The United States was treated in similar fashion:

The divergent development of Northerners and Southerners in America arose from contrasts in climate, soil and area. It was not only the enervating heat and moisture of the Southern States, but also the large extent of their fertile area which necessitated slave labour, introduced the plantation system, and resulted in the whole aristocratic organization of society in the South.[18]

Finally, and still in accordance with Ratzel, Semple notes that 'Nordic' peoples lose their energy and deteriorate when they migrate to the south. She points to the sorry state of Spanish, French and German colonists but says nothing about the British, whose colonial activity had exposed them to every type of climate.

It is time to summarize the main points. For Hippocrates and Ibn Khaldun, the ideal had been the temperate southern climate (the Mediterranean type). Jean Bodin had argued for a somewhat cooler temperate climate (on the same latitude as Paris). Montesquieu agreed with Bodin but exaggerated both the qualities of the north and the shortcomings of the south. This northward drift reached its apogee in the nineteenth century. In fact, it was not just a matter of a south–north drift but of a drift from the southeast to the northwest. The nomadic tribes of Siberia were doing themselves no favours by living on a higher latitude than the British. Nor, as we have seen, were the Russians. The much vaunted north was the north of the West. But while latitude provided a clear answer (for it matched the position of the great climatic zones), the role of longitude in the march of civilization remained more mysterious. The theory derived from an incontestable reality: the nucleus of modern civilization was situated in northwest Europe (and, from a certain moment, on the same latitudes on the opposite side of the Atlantic). But this situation had been produced by history, not by some immutable 'spirit of peoples' moulded by stifling heat or invigorating cold!

Climate and race, the two obsessions of the age, could be used to support different arguments. Some, like Gobineau and Chamberlain, saw race as the dominant element, while others privileged climate. Buckle believed that the concept of race was ambiguous and insufficient. But all the arguments led to the same conclusion: the superiority of the white population of temperate Europe. By extension, the combination of Nordic race and cool climate confirmed the superiority of northern Europe and its tall blonde race!

By combining the two factors, it was possible to arrive at a comprehensive interpretation of world history. This was the goal of the Romanian historian Alexandru D. Xenopol (1847–1920), whose voluminous *La Théorie de l'histoire*, published in Paris in 1908, enjoyed a certain critical success. Xenopol puts it bluntly:

> If the environment is favourable to development and if this environment is occupied by a superior race, the march of progress will be at its most energetic (as in Europe). When an average race is situated in a favourable environment, it may achieve a high degree of development (as in China and Japan). When, on the contrary, a superior race is relegated to a less favourable environment, its progress will be obstructed (as in India). If an inferior race is confined to an unfavourable environment, its progress will be almost completely destroyed (as with the Negroes of Africa).[19]

Any comment would be superfluous.

THE BLONDE GODS OF THE NORTH

The cold northern climate played an interesting role in German studies of prehistory before it entered Nazi mythology. At the centre of the debate were the Indo-Europeans, known as Indo-Germans in Germany, and later 'Aryans'. Their history had begun in the eighteenth century, with the observation of similarities between Greek, Latin and Sanskrit. In the following century several linguists, mostly German like Franz Bopp (1791–1867), surmised that a series of Asian and European languages – Sanskrit, Iranian, Greek, Latin, Celtic, Germanic, Slavic and others – had all stemmed from a single mother tongue. The next step was to identify the people who had spoken it. This was thought to have been an elite race that, through its descendants, had engendered the most highly developed civilizations on the planet. A people or a race also indicated a narrowly defined space of origin. Where had these mysterious Indo-Europeans come from? Attention initially focused on Central Asia, that cradle of so many civilizations. The Indo-Europeans then began to 'migrate', at the whim of scholars' fantasies but also for ideological reasons, as each nation sought to claim these prestigious ancestors as its own. They were forced to walk across a good part of Asia and Europe.

The first name that springs to mind in any discussion of Aryans or of modern racism in general is that of Count Arthur de Gobineau (1816–1882). Gobineau, author of *Essai sur l'inégalité des races humaines* (1853–5), was convinced that whites were superior to other races and Aryans superior to other whites. All the great civilizations (including China and Egypt) had been Aryan or had at least benefited from an infusion of Aryan blood. The Count was pessimistic about the future because of interbreeding, the Aryans themselves having lost their original purity. Gobineau adhered to the traditional view that all races, including Aryans, had originated in Central Asia. We should not expect to find much discussion of climate in his arguments. Climatic factors had little bearing on the genesis of the races. The white race, Gobineau explained, had originated on the plateaus of Central Asia, isolated from the rest of humanity by the high mountains on one side and on the other, towards the north, by ice fields. The harsh climate had probably contributed something to its unique qualities but, as other races had originated in similar conditions yet displayed no equivalent moral and intellectual development, Gobineau remained sceptical as to the effect of climate.[20]

Attempts to establish a link between Aryans and cold weather continued, however. Gustav Kossina (1858–1931), a renowned

German archaeologist, had more success (or perhaps did more damage) than any other prehistorian in harmonizing his important archaeological discoveries with a nationalist and even racist project. Whatever the case, it was goodbye to Central Asia. According to Kossina, the cradle of the 'Indo-Germans' was located in northern Europe and more precisely in Scandinavia, from where the 'Nordic race' had gradually spread across Europe and the Indo-Iranian half of Asia. The Nazis, great consumers of prehistoric mythology, enthusiastically adopted this schema. At a certain point during the ice age, northern Europe had been so cold that only the strongest had survived, producing an exceptional race: the Aryans. Unfortunately, as they moved away from their homeland they mingled with other races and their purity had been diluted. The Germans, fortunately, remained close to the primitive racial core.[21]

Moreover, it was not just the Germans who worshipped at the altar of the 'tall blonde race' and the 'great North'. A similar current of thought, encouraged by Madison Grant's *The Passing of the Great Race* (1916), sprang up in the United States. Grant also privileges the 'blonde race' of the Baltic region, the strongest, most intelligent and virtuous of all human groups. Its qualities derived from the climate; harsh winters and a host of other environmental difficulties had contributed to an extremely efficient process of human selection by eliminating the weak.[22]

The 'practical' consequences of such a theory are disturbing. Given a warmer climate, how can we ensure racial purity and superiority? Hitler had already found the answer.

GLACIERS, GRAPE HARVESTS AND CLIMATIC OSCILLATIONS

But perhaps climate had its own history. Perhaps, like humanity, it had also been subjected to changes and even revolutions.

Eighteenth-century thinkers were alert to this possibility. As nineteenth-century science delved more deeply into the natural world, it began to reveal the existence of climatic oscillations. The greatest excitement came from the discovery of the ice age. Scientists had long been intrigued by the rocky debris strewn across many parts of Europe. Louis Agassiz (1807–1873), a Swiss naturalist who settled in the United States, developed the theory that the debris had been transported in blocks of solid ice (*Etude sur les glaciers*, 1840). At some point in history, temperatures had plunged and the Earth had been 'covered by a vast sheet of ice'. If the theory was correct, it meant that climate too was susceptible to occasional and major variations.

Other oscillations, more recent and less dramatic, were identified. The Swiss were in an ideal position to observe the way Alpine glaciers advanced during cooling phases and retreated when it became warmer. Glaciological research had begun in the eighteenth century and had become much more precise by the early 1800s. Agassiz cites one of his precursors, Ignace Venetz, author of an 1833 essay on temperature variations in the Swiss Alps, based on fieldwork on the moraines (which indicated the variable limits of glaciers). Venetz had also scrutinized communal and parish registers, valuable sources of information on the masses of ice that posed such a threat Alpine communities. It seemed that areas that had been relatively ice-free between the eleventh and the fifteenth century had become less so in the seventeenth century and impassable in the next. It appeared that the glaciers were still advancing, a tendency confirmed by Agassiz.[23]

Towards the end of the nineteenth century, glaciology was complemented by another method that would become known as phenology, the study of plant development in relation to climatic phenomena. Variations in the ripening and flowering of plants should correspond with meteorological and climatic variations, but this type of data is not very reliable. There is, however, one striking exception: the dates of grape harvests, which had been scrupulously recorded for several centuries, particularly in France. In 1883, the French meteorologist Alfred Angot (1848–1924) published a study covering grape harvests from the sixteenth to the nineteenth centuries.[24] As the speed at which grapes ripen depends on temperature and other meteorological factors, the grape harvest period should provide a fairly accurate climatic profile of each year (although Angot did not rule out the intervention of other, non-meteorological factors).

The date palm also contributed something to climate history. It had flourished in Palestine in antiquity but its numbers had since diminished to the point of extinction. This indicated that the Mediterranean climate had been subject to variations.

Yet nineteenth-century climatologists were reluctant to draw firm conclusions from their data. According to many interpretations, the most pronounced variations could be attributed to local conditions. Agassiz believed that the advance and retreat of the Alpine glaciers was related to the Swiss climate and not to changes in the global climate. The now classic story of the medieval colonization of the Greenland coast was often cited. The venture had been launched under favourable climatic conditions but the colonists were eventually forced off the island as the weather deteriorated. But in this case too, the climatic oscillations were thought to be strictly regional. Moreover, as Agassiz himself remarks, the extension of the Alpine glaciers did not correspond with the Greenland cooling in chronological terms. Therefore, they had to be taken as separate phenomena: 'Despite the general stability of global temperature, local circumstances might have had a real and considerable effect on the climate in some countries.'[25]

The pattern is now clear: a prehistoric period subjected to major and global climatic variations (such as the ice age), and a recorded history affected by generally less pronounced and more regional variations.

From his study of grape harvests, Angot concluded that climatic conditions remain relatively stable although they may fluctuate from year to year or for longer periods. There was no evidence to suggest that climate had undergone change in the strict sense of the word: 'To summarize, the discussion of observations relating to the vine shows that the French climate has been prone to temporary oscillations, sometimes in one sense and sometimes in another, but on average it has not changed for fourteen or fifteen centuries.' Nor had the temperature in Greece and the eastern Mediterranean 'varied appreciably over the course of twenty-three centuries'. The same applied to China. All in all: 'the Earth's average climate has not appreciably changed since the beginning of recorded history.'[26]

Angot was expressing the generally accepted view of the day. The nineteenth century 'flirted' with the idea of climatic oscillations and prepared the ground for the more wide-ranging interpretations of the following century. Nevertheless, it firmly believed that climate had remained fairly constant since the end of the ice age, in other words, over the entire course of recorded history.

THE END OF THE SAHARA: *changing the climate at will*

Before taking our leave of the nineteenth century, we should consider its views on man's ability to modify climate. We have noted the highly optimistic considerations of Buffon and Gibbon on this topic. Their nineteenth-century successors generally displayed an even greater optimism (it was the age of science, technology and progress, after all) but some were more sceptical. Their doubts were also justified by science, which was in the process of maturing and should not be led astray by naïve enthusiasms.

For enthusiasm, we should look first to Charles Fourier (1772–1837). This famous utopian believed that climatic improvement went hand in hand with human improvement. When the entire human race is organized into *phalanstères* (self-sufficient social units), climatic conditions will become idyllic; the weather will settle down, global temperatures will stabilize and the cold regions will become warmer. 'When this era arrives, the entire world will be opened to agriculture, which will result in temperatures five to twelve degrees higher in still uncultivated latitudes like Siberia and northern Canada. The polar extremities will enjoy almost the same temperature as Andalucia and Sicily.' This spectacular process will be determined both by human activity (the spread of agriculture towards the poles) and cosmic factors: the intensification of the aurora borealis will ensure greater warmth and at the same time prevent climatic excesses. We might even be able to alter the axis of the globe, whose defective position is the cause of climate irregularities. One thing is certain, in an egalitarian society the climate will become equal as well![27]

A work of popular meteorology published in 1862 is slightly more moderate in tone but obviously takes its cue from Fourier:

> We believe that abnormal atmospheric phenomena can be modified by collective human action when it has become sufficiently advanced in terms of solidarity to undertake the cultivation of the globe's barren surfaces . . . Our planet, like any entity, is progressing from chaos to order. Great atmospheric disturbances are merely part of its embryonic period.

It was felt that human activity would inevitably modify global temperatures. One possible consequence might be a redistribution of the planet's electromagnetic currents: 'The northern Aurora could intensify and even become centres of heat – an additional power to melt the polar ice and restore to navigation the magnificent Boreal sea into which the great rivers of Asia flow.' Man should also transform the deserts, those 'scandals of nature' whose excessive heat was responsible for climatic instability: 'Will we ever manage to rid ourselves of these deserts? By covering them with abundant vegetation, we would modify their extreme temperatures.' The entire planet should be cleaned up; not just deserts but also 'wilderness' like marshes, heaths and steppes.

This is a very optimistic programme. But worries, and very prescient ones, sometimes came to the fore. Were we not in the process of rashly diminishing the surface covered in forest, while 'the daily burning of coal deposits increases the proportion of carbonic gas?'[28]

The article on 'Climat' in *La Grande Encyclopédie* had sounded the same drum: 'Climatology will not be content with improving weather forecasts for a given area; we can affirm that it will, to a certain extent, alter climates and will do so in the not too distant future.'[29]

Let us return to Jules Verne and the savage, disease-ridden Africa of *Cinq semaines en ballon*. One of the novel's heroes assures us that one day Africa will be different:

> These climates, so deadly to foreigners, will be purified by crop rotation and drainage; these sparse waters will be united in a common bed and form a navigable artery. The country we fly over will be richer, more fertile and more vital than any other; it will become a great kingdom and produce discoveries even more astonishing than steam power and electricity.[30]

Although some thought that the age of climatic redevelopment was almost imminent, Camille Flammarion's detailed study of the future *La Fin du monde* (1894) situated it towards the end of the third millennium. The envisaged solution centres on a combination of solar and thermal energy: 'The sun's rays were accumulated in summer and distributed during the winter and the seasons had almost disappeared, especially since boreholes had brought to the surface the seemingly inexhaustible heat contained within the planet's core.'[31]

It was a fine idea but it would probably take too long. Albert Robida (1848–1926) aimed to speed things up in his futuristic fantasy *La Vie électrique* (1892). The novel is set in 1955 but we learn that control of the weather had already begun in 1938, with the aid of huge power stations:

> Our electricians oppose the aerial currents of the north with more powerful counter-currents, engulfing them in the core of an artificial cyclone and bearing them to the Saharas of Africa and Asia, where they reheat and create fertility by their torrential rains. Thus have we reconquered the Saharas of Africa, Asia and Oceania; thus have we fertilized the Nubian sands and the burning wastes of Arabia.

In summer, warm currents are directed towards the Arctic Ocean. These measures succeed in creating temperate conditions in every part of the world; the seasons and climatic zones have virtually ceased to exist.[32]

Besides theorists and utopians there were men of action who pressed for immediate intervention. The creation of seas in areas that suffered from excessive heat and aridity, for example, would lower temperatures and encourage much-needed rainfall. In 1874, the French officer François Roudaire launched an audacious scheme to create an inland sea in Africa. This involved turning the Tunisian *chotts*, a vast basin in the south of the country, into an 8,200 km² sea fed by a canal to the Mediterranean. The principal aim – besides the opportunities it offered for transport – was to increase humidity and transform part of the Sahara into arable land. Ferdinand de Lesseps, the builder of the Suez Canal, was attracted by this new exploit and surveys began in 1883. It came to nothing in the end; the project was abandoned and the Sahara remained as arid as ever.[33]

Dreams were all very well but it was time to wake up. Alfred Angot was probably speaking for most meteorologists when he claimed (in *Traité élémentaire de météorologie*, 1899) that human intervention would have little impact on climate. Even the 'reforestation' and 'land clearance' advocated by Buffon and his successors seemed to have furnished nothing conclusive in climatic terms. Some change might indeed be possible if we acted on a greater scale. For example, if the entire Sahara were transformed into a sea, the ambient temperature would fall by 8 to 10 degrees centigrade. This was obviously utopian. On the other hand, a much smaller Saharan sea, like the one already considered, would yield absolutely nothing, not even a few localized showers. Changing the climate will 'always be beyond Man's power'. All we can hope for are very slight modifications affecting very limited areas.[34]

Wholesale change or no change at all: that was the view as 1900 approached. It was a far cry from the year 2000.

FOUR

The Changing Climate: The Twentieth Century

FROM DETERMINISM TO POSSIBILISM

As the twentieth century unfolded, the 'climatic tendency' encountered both obstacles and stimuli. The obstacles were scientific and ideological. Nineteenth-century racism and nationalism had blended perfectly with climatic interpretations; by the standards of the time, the synthesis was thought to be quite 'politically correct'. Things changed after 1900 and much more radically (given the horrors generated by racism and nationalism) after the Second World War. Racial and climatic interpretations did not necessarily go together any longer but there was still an undeniable link between them. Both essentially emphasized the superiority of the North and the West and the inferiority of the 'other' (for racial or climatic reasons or for a combination of the two) and presented the image of a rigidly hierarchical and fragmented humanity. Although this type of discourse would be embraced and exacerbated by the Nazis and a few other more or less deluded ideologues, its intellectual credibility gradually declined after the turn of the century. It was arrogant and not very intelligent.

The 'psychology of peoples', a discipline more or less justified by climate, also went into decline. What the nineteenth century had considered an entirely separate science, although connected to the nationalism of the era, finally disappeared. A whole branch of climatic interpretation collapsed, a lineage that had stretched from Hippocrates to the Nordic superman of the Nazis.

Ideology and science go together; one sustains the other in a reciprocal relationship. But history and the social sciences became much more sophisticated after 1900. How could a single and very simple cause like climate explain complex structures and developments? Moreover, the very system of 'causes' was being called into question. Influences, determinisms and the one-to-one relationship of cause and effect gave way to more subtle interpretations that acknowledged the interdependence of a multitude of factors. Science, so fine and straightforward an endeavour in its early days, was turning out to be more and more complicated.

Intensive study of 'primitive' peoples had brought to light the complex relationship between man and environment. It had long been thought that the physical environment had had direct and brutal effects on early humanity, in the initial stages of social construction. But, by the early 1900s, American anthropologists had already proved – in a way that was difficult to refute – that environment had nothing to do with it![1] Franz Boas (1858–1942), author of *The Mind of Primitive Man* (1911) and Robert H. Lowie (1883–1957), author of *Culture and Ethnology* (1917), provided many examples of populations living in similar environments but presenting very different patterns of behaviour. The Eskimos and the Chuchki of northeastern Siberia share the same Arctic environment but the former live by hunting and fishing while the latter base their economy on breeding reindeer. Moreover, 'igloos', the houses the Eskimos build from blocks of snow, are unknown to the Chukchi. At the other extreme, in the subtropical environment, Hottentots lead a pastoral life while Bushmen continue their traditional existence as hunters. Some peoples have domesticated animals but others have not done so, although they live in similar conditions. Moreover, domesticated animals are often used for different purposes. Reindeer, for example, may be used as meat and transport, or solely as a means of transport. In the latter case, the animal may be put into harness or mounted. However, common elements are sometimes found among tribes living in different environments. Nature imposes limits, of course: the peoples of Central Africa could not be expected to live in igloos, however refreshing they might find it. But the range of possibilities between these extremes is immense. Environment does not automatically explain culture. There is no typology linking a certain environment with a certain type of society. Nothing is imposed by geography or climate. Man takes his own decisions (although the range of possibilities open to him depend on the particular environment he inhabits).

We thus make the transition from geographical (and climatic) *determinism* to geographical (and climatic) *possibilism*. The French schools of geography and history played a significant role in this reorientation. Whereas Ratzel and Semple had acknowledged man's 'response' while insisting on the 'formative' action of nature, geographer Paul Vidal de la Blache (1845–1918) acknowledged the importance of the physical environment but stressed the active role of man in 'taking possession of' and transforming the environment. His posthumously published *Principes de géographie humaine* (1922) discusses the global distribution of humanity from this new perspective. Were there favourable or unfavourable climatic conditions which facilitated or discouraged the process of populating the planet? The geographer noted considerable demographic disparities in environmentally similar regions. Physical data aside, many other factors had to be taken into consideration in order to understand how human communities took root, even in regions that initially appeared to be totally inhospitable: 'The distribution of humanity cannot be explained by the value of the land. Anyone casting an expert eye over climates and soil compositions and trying to deduce the degree of human occupation from them would leave himself open to error.' There are no precise climatic or geographical rules, only 'constantly shifting and complex causes'.[2]

Lucien Febvre (1878–1956), founder (with Marc Bloch) of the 'new French history' (the *Annales* school), developed and refined La Blache's argument; his *La Terre et l'évolution humaine* (1922) makes a heartfelt plea for geographical possibilism. Febvre's principal targets are Ratzel and particularly Ellen Semple, whose unjustified simplifications he denounces on almost every page. What exactly does she mean by mountains? Mountainous regions are highly diverse. And what about islands? Is there such a thing as an insular typology? How can one compare two relatively close Mediterranean islands like Sicily and Corsica? Sicily has always been exposed to the currents and tides of human history; it is a meeting place, a synthesis of the most diverse cultures. Corsica, on the other hand, has isolated itself and looks towards the mountains of its interior rather than towards the sea. The same reasoning applies to climate. The physical environment offers a range of possibilities but the selection and exploitation of these possibilities belongs to man and society. There are no influences, only extremely complex relationships.

CLIMATE CHANGE AND HUMAN PROGRESS: *Huntington's system*

But climate had its allies as well as its enemies. As the cause of bitter scientific and ideological battles, it acquired new resources that revitalized it as a principle of historical interpretation. The fact is that a high level of 'sensitivity' to climate has persisted throughout the twentieth century and into our own time. In the eighteenth and nineteenth centuries, it was believed that technological progress would ultimately succeed in freeing man completely from the influence of nature. Towns in particular, 'artificial' spaces detached from the environment, were seen as offering their inhabitants protection from the hazards of the weather (whereas traditional rural societies, working to the rhythm of the seasons, were exposed to them). As we are now aware, that position was unrealistic. In fact, a double-edged process was under way: man was becoming both more powerful and more dependent. Population growth and density, especially in already overcrowded urban centres, creates new dependences sometimes more exacting than those experienced by traditional societies. Moreover, the risk of natural and technological disasters has intensified; think of the real or potential threats posed by earthquakes, nuclear accidents, floods, etc. Urban, industrial and agricultural demand for water is already creating problems. The vagaries of the weather expose the fragility of transport systems and other infrastructure. Heavy rain, snow and cold spells are always likely to produce disasters, or at least disruption. In some respects, the pre-industrial world enjoyed a greater degree of security: needs were less and the range of problems more limited. There was no risk of power cuts, failed heating systems or traffic jams.

There is no doubt that contemporary humanity is much more interested in how the economy works than in the distinctive traits of other peoples. And it is equally certain that economic activity is noticeably more closely linked to climate than to elusive national characteristics.

The problematic of history has altered considerably in relation to traditional approaches. The presumed connection between climate and the psychology of peoples and the formula 'climatic zones/zones of civilization' had been appropriate as long as the structures of history were thought to be virtually static. Certainly, history had had its ups and downs, but the human condition had undergone no essential change. But from the eighteenth century onwards, the 'structural' movement gradually came to the fore, casting doubt on traditional interpretations: thinkers were forced to agree that individuals and communities underwent marked changes from one era to the next. In terms of climate, it became more rewarding to address the global mechanism of history, to focus on the march of civilization rather than on an almost static tableau. Once history was on the move, climate had to move with it. Two things were thus brought into line: dynamic history and dynamic climate.

In short, we are dealing with a mental mutation that began in the eighteenth century and that subsequent generations would refine. It corresponds to the shift from a relatively stable world to a fluid world distinguished by and subject to increasingly rapid transformations. As a consequence, the 'fixity' that had dominated consciousness for so long was forced to yield to evolution and change. No exception could be made for climate, which began to emerge from its relative immobility. Although aware of climate oscillations as early as the nineteenth century, as we have observed, scholars remained sceptical about their extent and impact on history. The tone was to change after 1900.

A radical revision occurred in 1907, with the publication of Ellsworth Huntington's *The Pulse of Asia*, the result of several years' research in Central Asia. This is a significant date in climate history: for the first time, an ambitious and coherent theory of the climatic changes that might have determined the progress of humanity had been formulated. Huntington refined his theory in several later books, including *Civilization and Climate* (1915) and *Earth and Sun* (1923).

One of the American geographer's points of departure was clearly *L'Asie centrale* (1843), the work of the celebrated German naturalist Alexander von Humboldt (1769–1859). After conducting field studies and examining ancient local sources, Humboldt had concluded that in prehistoric times the vast bowl of Central Asia had been covered by a great inland sea that probably extended westward to the Black Sea and northward to the Arctic Ocean.[3] It was thought that the Caspian and Aral Seas were the two surviving 'fragments' of this original sea and had still been linked at the time of Herodotus (fifth century BC). The region had progressively dried up for reasons connected with climate or shifting ground levels. Huntington was intrigued by this idea and used his own geological and archaeological studies to refine and complete Humboldt's arguments. The ruins scattered over various desert sites seemed to offer proof that the climate had been much more favourable in antiquity than it is today.

Huntington concluded that the level of the Caspian Sea had been 150 feet (45 metres) higher at the time of Herodotus and Alexander the Great and had extended almost as far as the Aral Sea.[4] Three or four centuries later, at the beginning of the Christian era, its level had fallen by 50 feet (approximately 15 metres). His data, a rigorously constructed ensemble of climatic, environmental, human and historical factors, seems to provide a clear explanation for this change: in antiquity, the region had benefited from a cooler, wetter climate. The temperature had begun to rise and it had become progressively more arid, which accounted for both the fall in sea levels and the decline of once-flourishing civilizations like Persia, which had been eroded by desertification.

But the impact of climatic changes in Asia had even greater consequences. The drop in the level of the Caspian Sea and the fall of the Roman Empire are two aspects of the same phenomenon. As Central Asia became drier, its populations were forced to seek more humid and fertile lands elsewhere. People began to move en masse, creating the great migrations that spread across Europe and eventually brought about the fall of the Roman Empire and the collapse of ancient civilization.

This climatic model extends beyond Asia. According to Huntington the climate has, as a general rule, become steadily hotter and drier since the last ice age. Like the changes in Central Asia, the desertification of the northern half of the African continent (the Sahara) had occurred fairly recently. The earliest civilizations, Egypt and Mesopotamia, had crystallized in a climate similar to that of Europe today. In other words, civilizations had migrated northwards as the south became hotter and drier. Human progress had always been stimulated by the same set of climatic conditions. The theory holds out little hope for hot countries. The exceptional position of Egypt could be explained by the fact that it had enjoyed similar climatic conditions to those that prevail in modern Britain (although the British climate had been almost arctic when ancient Egypt was flourishing!).[5]

Huntington's own summary of his theory of world history is succinct: 'long-continuing changes of climate have been one of the controlling causes of the rise and fall of the great nations of the world'.[6] The mechanism may differ from case to case but the climate always plays its part. If we look beyond Central Asia and the Roman Empire, we find that the wave of epidemics that destroyed the first Mayan Empire were also due to climatic disturbances.

Huntington's methodology drew on many sources. His definition of the ideal climate, a *single* climate favourable to the process of civilization, owes a great deal to E. G. Dexter's *Weather Influences* (1904). Dexter did not attempt to explain human progress through climate; his study focused on the reactions of specific groups of people – schoolchildren, criminals and bank staff – to variations in the weather. He noted that excessive humidity diminished energy, while dryness combined with heat induced a state of nervousness that went as far as loss of self-control. The most stimulating conditions were those offered by cool and moderately dry (or moderately humid) weather. Huntington apparently considered these localized observations a sufficient basis on which to erect a philosophy of history: high-performance civilizations evolved in a climate that was neither too cold and wet nor too hot and dry or, more precisely, one that did not induce either depressive or manic behaviour.

The great movements of history may be stimulated by climate change but smaller-scale events are often due to the caprices of the weather. Huntington notes a characteristic sequence in several countries (particularly Central Asia and the domains of the Ottoman Empire): lack of rain – food shortages – inability to pay taxes – social unrest – insurrections, wars and massacres. Even in the wealthier and more civilized United States, 'each of the great financial crises of the country has been associated with a deficiency of rainfall' (a quotation from an article by H. H. Clayton with the edifying title 'Influence of Rainfall on Commerce and Politics', 1902).[7] In the United States, poor harvests, higher prices and popular discontent do not lead to massacres and wars but to political crises which may result in altered congressional majorities or in presidential elections. If rainfall is such a dominant factor in politics, how can we doubt that climatic excesses trigger much more radical changes?

CHALLENGE AND RESPONSE: *history according to Toynbee*

Of all the twentieth-century theories of civilization, Arnold J. Toynbee's massive *A Study of History* (12 volumes, 1934–61) is undoubtedly the most impressive (although, like any system, it aroused considerable controversy). Toynbee is too meticulous a historian to rely exclusively on climate. He admires Huntington's work but has a better grasp of the complexity of historical phenomena. Even so, as a 'system-builder' he goes much further than his French colleague Lucien Febvre, whose 'possibilism', when projected to infinity, cancelled out the very idea of 'typology' or 'system'. Toynbee's preferred mechanism can be summarized

in two words: 'challenge' and 'response'. Civilizations are responses to the challenges posed by a variety of natural and human
'obstacles'.

Climate does play a relatively important role in this theory,
particularly climate change, which causes shocks and thus pro-
vokes responses. Citing V. Gordon Childe's *The Most Ancient East*,
Toynbee bases his interpretation of the origins of the first civilizations on the 'gradual desiccation' of the Middle East and southern
Mediterranean in the period following the last ice age.[8] This
climatic challenge stimulated some of the region's communities
into changing their habitat and way of life. They settled on the
banks of great rivers and founded the Egyptian and Sumerian
civilizations. As we can see, the causal factor – drought – is close
to Huntington's, but the mechanism is different. Toynbee believes
in the positive effects of hardship: if there were no difficulties to
be overcome, there would be no such thing as civilization.

In order to constitute the founding principle of a civilization, the
challenge must be sufficiently powerful (so that it provides the
necessary stimulus) but not so powerful that it crushes the human
groups affected by it. Scotland is a harsher country than England.
Consequently, the response of its inhabitants has been more
intense: 'The popular impression that the Scots have played a part
disproportionate to their numbers in the making of the British
Empire and in the occupancy of the high places of church and
state is undoubtedly well founded.'[9] Their 'superiority' has been
fostered by climate and environment. In North America, the New
England colonists, who had chosen to live in the most hostile corner of the continent, eventually prevailed over the French, Spanish
and Dutch who had settled in more favourable regions. In short,
Anglo-Saxon supremacy in North America had been made easier,
although not determined, by environment and climate.[10] The
greatest achievements of Scandinavian civilization were seen not in

Norway, Sweden or Denmark but in Iceland, where the Vikings had successfully adapted to appreciably harsher natural and climatic conditions. But the next 'leap', to Greenland, where conditions were even worse than those in Iceland, had failed. Attempts to settle the Greenland coast had eventually been defeated by an environment that had proved to be more powerful than man.[11]

CLIMATE HISTORY: METHODS, RECONSTRUCTIONS AND INTERPRETATIONS

Huntington's work on the effects of climate change, although innovative and impressive, was simplistic. His interpretations were based on fragmentary and dubious data. Moreover, his over-deterministic view of climate ignored the existence of an intricate network of historical factors. Subsequent generations adopted a more nuanced and pragmatic approach. Instead of constructing broad outlines from minimal data, they focused on a patient reconstruction of climate history itself. They also avoided deterministic preconceptions; while climate was the principal object of study, it was situated in a complex, interdependent system in which man and society represented the most dynamic agents.

The starting point therefore had to be the 'invention' of climate history in as complete and reliable a form as possible. The project was stimulated by the almost simultaneous appearance of two models of research that were to become classics of their kind. In 1966, the British climatologist H. H. Lamb published *The Changing Climate*. The following year, Emmanuel Le Roy Ladurie, a French historian with wide-ranging interests, published his *Histoire du climat depuis l'an mil* (translated into English in 1971 under the title *Times of Feast, Times of Famine: A History of the Climate Since the Year 1000*). While Le Roy Ladurie's later work addressed other aspects of history in which climate featured only incidentally, Lamb went on to produce further contributions to the field, notably *Climatic History and the Future* (1977–85) and *Climate, History and the Modern World* (1982; second edition 1995). These seminal texts generated a body of research that brought together historians and climatologists in a major interdisciplinary endeavour.

The invention of climate history required the invention of a new methodology. It was primarily a problem for the imagination. No other field of historical research had imposed such demands on the imagination or the capacity for methodological innovation. This approach, a radical contrast to the caution of traditional methods (which were usually confined to the study of written sources) would act as a stimulus in every field of historical research.

Where, in fact, were the sources of climate history to be found? Meteorological records did exist but they were fairly recent (the first observations using instruments were made in England and France towards the end of the seventeenth century; more detailed series for Europe were compiled in the eighteenth). Written sources of all kinds – archival material, chronicles and diaries (particularly from the Middle Ages) – were rich in meteorological information that had received scant attention before the advent of climate history. Such records had been the object of careful study for several decades since then but could not be expected to provide a complete and rigorous overview (medieval 'weather reports' were chiefly concerned with deviations from the norm in winter temperatures and summer rainfall). The difficulty lay in finding objective and precise indicators comparable with modern meteorological instruments.

The problem was addressed from several angles. Existing methods could be perfected: the Alpine glaciers, for example are highly sensitive indicators and had been under observation for at least two hundred years. If the temperature rises by one degree glaciers recede towards the peaks; if it falls by one degree they advance deep into the valleys, threatening the villages in their path. These phases can be established from written accounts and field studies conducted on moraines, including radiocarbon dating of vegetable matter preserved in the ice, a procedure unavailable to Agassiz. Le Roy Ladurie had the idea of comparing eighteenth-century engravings of Alpine glacial landscapes with recent photographs of the same sites. His study reveals that the glaciers had receded perceptibly over the course of the last two centuries, indicating recent rises in temperature.

The 'glaciological' approach encompasses much more sophisticated techniques. Scientists turned their attention to the Antarctic and Greenland ice caps and made a breakthrough in 1966, when a 1,390 metre-long core sample was extracted from the Greenland icecap. Further extractions were carried out, as chemical analysis of this kind of ice, which has accumulated over the ages and forms a complete archive of climate, yields conclusive data on the climatic profile over successive periods.

Grape harvests, already investigated by Angot, were not forgotten. Le Roy Ladurie re-examined the data compiled by his predecessor (a distinctively French approach, one might say), and came to rather different conclusions, finding more clearly defined variations that lent further credence to the theory of climatic periodization.

Tree-felling, an activity not previously associated with the methodologies of history or climatology, also played its part. As early as 1900, A. E. Douglas of the University of Arizona had embarked upon this kind of research, founding the science of 'dendroclimatology' in the process. Douglas benefited from ideal conditions: Arizona has a particularly arid climate and contains very old trees such as bristlecone pines, which help to highlight deviations from the norm. The principle is simple (although as with anything, it is simple once you know how). Tree trunks show concentric growth rings and a new ring is added each year. A historian, even a mathematician, can make a mistake when working with figures but there is no such risk with a tree – the number of its rings corresponds exactly with its age. The rings are not identical, however, their development depends on the meteorological profile, favourable or unfavourable, of the year in question, a pattern that obviously invites interpretation. In Arizona, a favourable year, broadly speaking, would be wetter than the norm, but in Scandinavia, where the problem is one of cold rather than rainfall, it would be warmer. Tree-dating thus affords an insight into the history of the climate over hundreds or even, in the case of a bristlecone pine, thousands of years.

The range of investigative methods available also includes the study of fossilized pollen (vestiges of plant life, which in turn depends on climate), the analysis of various types of sediment (which throws light on the vegetal and climatic context of each period) and the study of coral reefs (which provides evidence of variations in sea level). Anything related in one way or another to climate is worthy of study. As a final example, fluctuations in cereal prices reflect harvest yield, which is, in turn, subject to the vagaries of the weather.[12]

All these sources of information have been carefully analysed and provide us with a complete and detailed history of the climate. It seems that we know more about what the weather was like in a precise place and at a precise moment a few centuries ago than about how it will behave in a few weeks' time. I will briefly sketch the principal stages.[13]

After the last ice age, temperatures rose to a 'climatic optimum' in the Neolithic era. This optimum, sometimes called the 'sunny millennium', occurred between 4,000 and 3,000 BC, when an average temperature 2°C above the current level seems to have encouraged the spread of primitive agriculture. Antiquity entered a cooler period marked by successive colder and warmer spells. A warm phase occurred during the Middle Ages, toward the end of the first millennium. This reached its peak in Greenland in the twelfth century and continued to affect Europe until about 1300. When the Vikings settled on the Greenland coast the country was apparently still 'green', and its name had yet to acquire ironic overtones. A new phase of cooling set in (by the thirteenth century the Greenland settlers were already retreating before the cold) and continued, interrupted by warmer episodes, until the middle of the sixteenth century, when the Little Ice Age began.

Historians and climatologists have examined the well-documented Little Ice Age in great detail. It has provided irrefutable evidence that climate is subject to significant variations and that it affects economy and society. It also lasted a remarkably long time – three hundred years, from the middle of the sixteenth century to perhaps the late nineteenth century, a span marked by warmer or colder sub-periods. Some authors suggest that it began two or three hundred years earlier, immediately after the preceding 'optimum', and have sometimes placed it within a very precise chronological framework, from 1303 to 1859. Alpine glaciers advanced considerably during the Little Ice Age. Winters were extremely harsh, particularly between 1690 and 1699; ice bridges formed over European rivers, including the Mediterranean part of the Rhône, while the Thames froze eleven times in the seventeenth century and twenty times between 1564 and 1814. This makes it easier to understand Napoleon's disastrous campaign in Russia and the terrible, abnormally early winter that destroyed the French army. And it also throws light on the climatic context of *Frankenstein*. Mary Shelley wrote her novel while staying with Shelley and Byron near Geneva in the summer of 1816. A cold rain fell incessantly and she and her companions were confined to their villa, huddled over a constantly burning fire. It was the coldest summer ever recorded in Europe.

About the mid-nineteenth century, temperatures began to rise (the ever-sensitive Alpine glaciers immediately responded by retreating to the mountain tops). This continues today and is apparently intensified by the greenhouse effect, which will be discussed later. (These major stages are themselves divided into sub-periods with their own varying climatic profiles – they may be hotter or colder in relation to the global context and, at the same time, may also be characterized by regular annual fluctuations.)

Is this schema above suspicion? I would suggest that no version of history is above suspicion. History is never 'true' in the absolute sense of the word. Or, to put it a better way, the only absolutely true history is the history that has actually occurred. But what we usually refer to as 'history', i.e., the reconstruction of the past, can only be a simplified, fragmentary and biased undertaking. The problem begins with the sources themselves, which are not 'realities' but more or less incomplete and distorted reflections of a certain historical reality. Second, history is a matter of the historian's gaze or, more generally, of the way each era regards its past (which is inevitably through the eyes of the present).

To return to climate history, the proliferation of new methods should not be allowed to disguise a certain amount of approximation. No thermometer will tell us the average temperature for the year 1300. We have to combine data gleaned from contemporary accounts, glaciers, tree trunks and other sources to arrive at an approximate calculation. The climatologist constructs a model; his figures are 'created' from a mixture of partly subjective and very often indirect indicators. While he may succeed in sticking close to reality, it would be unrealistic to expect a flawless reconstruction. If the precisely measured changes occurring in our own century are the object of dispute, what can we expect from measurements of past climatic behaviour? One account will tell us that the history of the Roman Empire, for example, corresponded to a warm phase while another will claim that it spanned a colder period. The first centuries of the Middle Ages (before the advent of the 'little climatic optimum') present us with the same choice: warm or cold?[14]

We are justified in wondering if data derived from tree-rings or glaciers is as valuable as that provided by the sophisticated instruments meteorologists use today. It has been observed, for example, that the growth of tree-rings depends not only on temperature but on a wide range of other factors, which introduces a degree of relativity into the conclusions. Moreover, growth occurs principally during the summer months, influenced by the hours of daylight, which tends to sideline the effects of the cold season. Similarly for grape harvests, how far do they depend on strictly meteorological factors, given the number of other factors? The various sources examined and methods employed apply to land masses, while 70 per cent of the Earth's surface is covered by ocean. Moreover, most of the data has been drawn from a selective sampling of parts of North America and Western Europe, which further restricts the scope of the domain under study.[15] There is a danger of constructing generalizations from fragmentary regional data. The global climate is a synthesis and to some extent an abstraction; it is a composite of many regional climates and their evolutions are not inevitably identical.

Climate historians have coined two terms that have exacerbated our tendency to dramatize the climate changes of the last thousand years. These are the 'medieval warm period', which applies to the first three centuries of the millennium, and the 'Little Ice Age'. The latter has a particularly impressive ring to it: it evokes, although on a smaller scale, the true ice ages of the Quaternary. Despite the popularity of these labels, climatologists have recently suggested that temperatures in the northern hemisphere were not subject to major fluctuations (their revised temperatures are 'invented' from all sorts of indications, of course; but everything in this domain has to be invented). The most authoritative figures, advanced by M. E. Mann and his collaborators (1999), 'record' an average difference of no more than 0.4°c between the warmest medieval period and the coldest modern period. Other estimates are a little more generous but none venture higher than one degree and most tend to register about half a degree.[16]

This may seem surprisingly low, but we are assured that even one degree is on the high side, particularly if we are dealing with major changes like the advance of glaciers and the extension or retreat of cultures according to altitude or shifts towards the north. Moreover, it is obvious that it is simply a question of averages resulting from quite different situations. An average rise of 0.5°c can be expressed by an increase of 2–3°c in a determined region. This was apparently the case in Greenland during the medieval 'warm' period. But if averages are to be respected, truly significant changes should be matched by more stable situations, or even changes that have entirely the opposite effect.

Some scientists now tend to play down the scale of temperature change. It may be, for example, that the 'medieval warm period' was a localized phenomenon and did not extend much beyond the north Atlantic region. However, these reputedly 'warm' or 'cold' periods were marked by significant variations. Cold spells were not uncommon in the 'climatic optimum', nor were heatwaves in the middle of the Little Ice Age. The seventeenth century witnessed some particularly harsh winters but also some very hot summers. The end of the eighteenth century, far from being 'glacial' as the model suggests, was marked by a rather warm climate . . . and so it goes on. Recent research has shown that apart from some undeniably low temperatures, the Little Ice Age was characterized by irregular weather patterns that frequently fluctuated from one extreme to the other. It becomes legitimate to wonder if these climatic 'periods' actually existed as coherent, clearly defined and objective divisions. Everything boils down to a question of outlook and interpretation. When Le Roy Ladurie examined Angot's series of grape harvests, he saw what Angot himself had refused to see: a succession of distinct climatic periods.

The reconstruction of climate history poses many problems but the interpretation of its relationship to the history of humankind is even more open to controversy. Determinism is no longer in fashion but every new historical approach, as cautious as it may be in theoretical terms, offers temptations to which historians – always on the lookout for 'causes' and explanations – will occasionally succumb. There is a tendency for metaphorical labels like the 'medieval warm period' and the Little Ice Age to be taken literally.

Several historians and climatologists have integrated the climatic factor – rising temperatures – into the interpretation of one of the most important turning points in history: the 'taking-off' of the Western world after the first millennium (the distant but effective point of departure for today's technological civilization). Indeed, how can we explain the genesis of a civilization that turned out to be so different from others? Obviously, no one person holds the key to this process. But as ever, historians have applied themselves to listing the real or presumed causes. Climate, without becoming determinant, sometimes occupies a prominent position. Climatic changes may have favoured the expansion of agriculture, the economic base that kick-started the rise of the West. H. H. Lamb remarks that characteristic examples of sustained 'social energy' like the great period of cathedral-building and the Crusades, correspond with a period of maximum warmth in Europe.[17] One degree more and we might have seen cathedrals rising in Greenland! On the other hand, the cold winters and poor (or occasionally extremely hot) summers of the Little Ice Age are blamed for bad harvests, famines and social unrest. Weather has also been cited as one of the causal factors of the French revolution – the unusually hot and dry summer of 1788 was followed by a very cold winter, conditions that had an impact on agricultural production and the collective mentality.[18]

All we can really say is that when it comes to 'causes', everything is a matter of choice. A choice, moreover, that depends as much on ideology and fashion as on science. And since the study of climatic change is fashionable, it would be unthinkable for historians to ignore these new accessories.

Let us take a brief look at the curve of interpretations. The determinist excesses of the nineteenth century gave way to a certain scepticism – perhaps Mother Nature was not as dominant as had once been thought. But, as time went on, several new elements contributed to a re-evaluation of the role played by the environment: nostalgia for a world marginalized and ruined by the abuses of technological civilization; the rise in ecological awareness and anxiety over the scale of environmental and climatic disasters. The context favoured historical and sociological interpretations that integrated 'space', 'nature' and 'climate' into their methodology. In this respect, nothing is more instructive than to compare Lucien Febvre and his disciple Fernand Braudel, respectively the most authoritative representatives of the first and second generations of 'new French history'. When it comes to man's relationship with the natural world, Febvre breaks with all typology and refuses to admit that any single evolutionary process is inevitable. Conversely, Braudel, in his fundamental *La Méditerranée et le monde méditerranéen à l'époque de Philippe II* (1949), sees in the Mediterranean area a physical unit which has quite specifically marked the civilizations that developed there. Braudel was one of the first historians to highlight the importance of the study of climatic variations. He went even further (almost as far as Huntington) in supposing that climate had played a decisive part in some of the turning points in human history. In his second great work, *Civilisation matérielle, économie et capitalisme* (first volume 1967, republished with two additional volumes in 1979), he suggests that climate change may have determined the generalized demographic expansion identified in the eighteenth century. This is a rather imprudent supposition: how did this climatic variation manifest itself and in what way did it act on demographic changes? Braudel remains silent on this and for good reason; he does no more than throw a stone in the pond.[19]

Meanwhile, the methods and conclusions of climate history have undergone considerable refinement and historians have learned to be more cautious. But the real or imaginary 'climatic pressure' felt by the societies of today will always be reflected in interpretations of history.

THE NORTH–SOUTH DIVIDE: *a return to Montesquieu?*

Social and economic imbalances, particularly the north–south divide, feature prominently among the developments that invite reinterpretation. These disparities had traditionally been explained through the effects of contrasting climates, a fatalistic view which argues that some regions of the globe are inherently privileged (Europe, the West, the North) and condemns others to a diminished existence (especially the 'hot countries'). Although this view has gradually been discarded, the gap between the richest and poorest countries continues to expand. Where can we find an explanation for this perverse development?

The problem is usually approached from a politico-economic angle that tends to incriminate either the West (globalization, unfair trade and insufficient aid), or the poor countries themselves (authoritarian regimes, corruption and bad economic management).

But geography and climate have come back into the equation, as in David S. Landes's *The Wealth of the World and Poverty of Nations. Why Some are so Rich and Some so Poor* (1998). This American economic historian has no hesitation in claiming that the human body is less able to tolerate heat than cold. The inhabitants of hot countries work less; the function of slavery was to make some do the work that others found too hard: 'it is not by chance that slave labour has been historically associated with tropical and semi-tropical climates'. This interpretation is very close to Montesquieu's. There are many other disadvantages, not least the damage wrought by tropical diseases. On the other hand, Europe, especially the northwest, has been privileged in climatic terms (temperate climate, sufficient rainfall, the alternating seasons, the moderating effect of the Gulf Stream, etc.). Why then did the development of Western Europe lag behind the civilizations of the East? The explanation is still geographical: vast forests of broad-leaved trees initially hindered the development of populations and cultures. Was this a case of geographical inevitability? Not altogether, because other properly human factors intervened over the course of history and will continue to do so in the future. Even so, it would be imprudent to ignore or play down the existence of essential geo-climatic data. Here we have geography and climate rehabilitated as the foundations of human history.[20]

A NEW SOCIETY DEMANDS A NEW CLIMATE: *communism and water*

We may recall Robida's prediction that by the middle of the twentieth century man would be in complete control of the Earth's climate and able to change it 'at will'. We have not measured up to Robida's expectations. Any effect we have had on climate has been inadvertent and counter-productive: technological man is poisoning the atmosphere. Making the deserts bloom still seems beyond our capabilities. All we have achieved, or tried to achieve, is a little hopelessly localized artificial rain. We have used rockets or aircraft to 'seed' clouds with substances that can condense water vapour but scientists remain sceptical about the effectiveness of this process. Yet the determination to regularize climate has not diminished. It is just one of Western civilization's many scientific, technological and voluntarist projects designed to conquer and transform the world. Who is to say it will not happen tomorrow?

The creation of artificial inland seas has often been proposed as a method of tempering the tropical climate and putting an end to the ecological scandal represented by deserts. We have noted the failure of the Saharan sea project. In the early 1900s, Australian scientists devised several purely theoretical schemes to enlarge Lake Eyre (at the centre of the continent, in the middle of the desert), either by means of a canal leading south to the Spencer Gulf or by the adduction of the waters of several rivers. There too, the uncertainty of the results tempered enthusiasm and this enterprise effectively sank into obscurity.

The most enthusiastic exponent of geographico-climatic development was a German engineer named Hermann Sergel. Two of his schemes went far beyond anything that human imagination had yet conceived in this area. The first, proposed in 1928, recommended nothing less than the draining of the Mediterranean. The idea had an appealing simplicity: two dams, one at Gibraltar and the other at the Dardanelles, would prevent the incursion of water from the Atlantic and the Black Sea. As the Mediterranean did not receive adequate replenishment from its own watercourses, it would diminish year by year and fall by 100 metres in the course of a century. This would create another 150,000 km² of dry land; the Adriatic would disappear and the boot of Italy would join up with North Africa. It is hard to see the utility of the project (the foreseeable ecological and climatic consequences of such enormous change would inspire us with horror today). It was probably just a case of man flexing his technological muscles, a suggestion that nothing was beyond his power.

Sergel came up with a new project in 1935. This time he suggested flooding the Belgian Congo by building a huge dam that would trap the river's waters and create a vast sea covering an area of 800,000 km². A feeder canal to the Sahara would then supply another artificial body, the 1,300,000 km² Sea of Chad. A 'second Nile' would emerge from the latter and flow into the Mediterranean. This would lead to the disappearance of the Sahara desert and the radical modification of climatic conditions in the northern half of Africa. The Belgian Congo would be wiped off the map, of course, but everything in this world has a price.

The West did not seem to be short of ideas but it was hesitant about putting them into practice. Russia was a very different case. Communist doctrine proclaimed the absolute triumph of man over history, the physical world and his own nature. Such ambitions, grounded in an already ancient vein of Western 'transformist' thought, were exacerbated by the doctrine of the 'radiant future'. Nothing could resist the advance of the 'new man' and the 'new society'; Fourier's great scheme had not been forgotten. This belief was explicitly stated by Trotsky in a text from 1924:

The current position of mountains, rivers, fields and meadows, steppes, forests and coasts cannot be considered permanent. Man has already wrought significant changes on the map of nature; they are simple schoolboys' exercises compared with what will come . . . Man will draw up a new inventory of the mountains and rivers . . . He will, probably, remodel the land according to his taste.[21]

The enormity and variety of the Russian landscape was perfectly suited to the highly voluntarist and transformist aspects of communist doctrine. The rapid transformation of a country that lagged behind in technological development required spectacular effort. Space was not a problem: the country was so vast it could encompass the most ambitious experiments. Climate featured among the regime's major objectives. Indeed, climatic conditions in Russia were even worse than socio-economic conditions and constituted another argument, or even an excuse, for the country's retarded development. The new Russia demanded a new climate. Most of its territory was afflicted by every climatic evil imaginable: the lands to the north of European Russia and Siberia were frozen; even the temperate zone was subject to marked climatic contrasts; central Asia was extremely arid while western Siberia was so saturated it formed an immense swamp. All that had to be changed.

The initial plan was for a series of canals linking the rivers and seas. The Baltic-White Sea Canal was opened in 1933, the Moscow-Volga Canal in 1937 and the Volga-Don Canal in 1952. Attention then turned to inland seas. Rivers were to be retained by massive dams and allowed to flood a considerable part of the Russian plain. The project was partially carried out: a glance at recent maps of Russia is enough to reveal several very large bodies of water. The most remarkable of these, the Rybinsk Sea to the north of Moscow, extends over 4,500 km²; several towns and hundreds of villages disappeared beneath its surface. Besides facilitating transport and irrigation, the inland seas were designed to modify climate by encouraging rainfall and moderating extreme weather patterns. The West had a similar programme and constructed its own canals, dams and artificial lakes, with inevitable consequences for the environment. What distinguishes communism, in this respect, is the sheer scale of the projects and the ideological imperative to transform the 'old order'.

Moreover, these projects were only the beginning; a much brighter future lay ahead. One scheme in particular was designed to bring about a sudden change in the environment and climate of Central Asia and the western half of Siberia, a region almost as big as Europe. The idea was to reduce humidity in western Siberia and increase it in Central Asia, where the naturally arid climate had further deteriorated due to the drying-up of the Aral Sea, a consequence of irrigation and other hydraulic works affecting its tributaries, the Amudar'ya and the Syrdar'ya. The operation was surprisingly simple, on paper at least. All engineers had to do was to construct a dam, 80 metres high and 50 kilometres long, which would block the course of the Ob, Siberia's longest river. This would lead to the formation of the Siberian Sea, an expanse of water covering 250,000 km². Another dam on the Yenizei would create an additional basin. An 800 kilometre-long canal complete with branches (in fact a new river with a discharge greater than the Volga) would channel the Siberian waters towards the tributaries of the Aral Sea. The steppes and deserts of Central Asia would thus be transformed into agricultural land, while the west Siberian swamplands, relieved of their surplus water, would become an agricultural region. Fortunately, this upheaval (the brainchild of the engineer Mitrofan Davydov) never took place, probably because the means to achieve it did not exist. By abandoning the scheme, the Soviets avoided even greater environmental degradation than the drying up of the Aral Sea. The people who proposed to transform the world had not even heard of the word 'ecology'.

Could Soviet engineers create, or at least conceive of, something even more ambitious? Of course, all the more because cold was as much their enemy as drought or excessive rainfall. The communist paradise was far from being the perpetual spring of the biblical paradise – in Cuba, perhaps, but not in Russia! Much of the Soviet Union lies above the Arctic Circle and even at lower latitudes the winters are extremely severe. How could the country be warmed up? In the research institutes, the experts set to work. The engineer Markine came up with a project: 'By using hundreds of giant pumps powered by the atomic energy from a three-million-kilowatt power station, we could empty the waters of the Pacific into the cold Arctic Ocean. We would thus create a warm current comparable to the Gulf Stream, which would then exercise a benevolent influence over the whole of northeast Siberia. The climate and vegetation of this region would be transformed.' The engineer P. M. Borisov suggested a variation designed to produce the same result. They could dam the Bering Straits and pump water from the Arctic Ocean into the Pacific. The reduced sea level would draw the warm waters of the Atlantic into the Arctic basin and melt the ice. Every part of Russia would experience climate change. In Moscow, the average winter temperature would rise to 8–12 degrees centigrade, putting it on a par with Athens or Rome. The Black Sea was not forgotten either. Some engineers advocated the construction of a dam linking the mouths of the Danube to the Crimea. At the same time they would cut through the Crimean isthmus and separate the Sea of Azov from the Black Sea. The waters of the Danube, Dniestr, Boug, Dnieper and Don rivers would be retained in the Sea of Azov and the northern part of the Black Sea. The Sea of Azov would be transformed into an immense fresh-water reservoir, another victory over aridity. The warm waters of the Mediterranean would make up the deficit in the greater part of the Black Sea, while temperatures in neighbouring regions would rise considerably.

These are the most advanced points that man has yet reached in his struggle, real or imaginary, to subdue nature and reinvent the world.[22]

FIVE

The Logic of the Flood

THE WRATH OF THE GODS

For a long time, the weather was the preserve of the gods; they used it to punish or reward human beings, or simply to pass the time. Jupiter–Zeus, head of the family of Greco-Roman gods, was responsible for thunder and lightning. In the Andaman Islands of the Indian Ocean, the domains of the supreme god are even more specific: his voice is the thunder, his breath the wind and the hurricane expresses his anger. Weather is almost always present in myths of origin; it appears throughout the legendary traditions of primitive, ancient and medieval cultures.[1]

For Jews and Christians, the God of the Bible also occasionally speaks in meteorological language. When he wished to punish humans, he created the Flood; when he wished to reward them, he sent manna from heaven. Even common phenomena like snow, rain and wind were examples of divine intervention, designed to lend greater emphasis to God's messages to mankind. God's appearance to Moses on the mountain has an essentially meteorological setting:

And it came to pass on the third day in the morning, that there were thunders and lightnings, and a thick cloud upon the mount, and the voice of the trumpet exceeding loud . . .

And mount Sinai was altogether on a smoke, because the LORD descended upon it in fire: and the smoke thereof ascended as the smoke of a furnace, and the whole mount quaked greatly. And when the voice of the trumpet sounded long, and waxed louder, Moses spake, and God answered him by a voice.[2]

When the Jews later settled in the Promised Land, their 'contract' with God included a specifically meteorological clause. As long as they remained faithful to the Creator he would make the rain fall regularly, ensuring that his people had sufficient food. If they strayed from the true path, however, the rain would stop. Another passage from the Bible is particularly explicit: 'Also by watering he wearieth the thick cloud: he scattereth his bright cloud. And it is turned round about by his counsels: that they may do whatsoever he commandeth them upon the face of the world in the earth. He causeth it to come, whether for correction, or for his land, or for mercy.'[3] Meteorology has no relevance in paradise, the place of perpetual spring. Rain is unnecessary as the paradisaical fountain assures the irrigation of the garden. Meteorology and its turbulences came after the Fall, adding another element to the uncertainty of the human condition.

At a certain stage in history, science began to compete with the gods in the interpretation of natural phenomena. The Greeks produced a classic analysis of the weather, Aristotle's *Meteorologica*, a text that would remain the standard reference on the subject for two thousand years, until the beginning of the modern era. The philosopher explained atmospheric phenomena by the action of the sun, which causes 'exhalations' as it heats the Earth's surface. Some of these exhalations, resulting from evaporation, are moist; others, composed of terrestrial particles, are dry. The former are the origin – according to temperature and place – of dew, rain and snow, while the latter give birth to the winds. Exhalations interact with the four elements – earth, air, fire and water – each of which has its own qualities, earth being cold and dry, water cold and wet, air wet and warm and fire hot and dry. The theory may not be accurate but the approach is distinctly scientific.

Isidore of Seville (*c.* AD 560–636) and the Venerable Bede (*c.* AD 672–735) were the meteorological authorities of the early medieval period. Employing elements of ancient lore, they attempted to explain and predict the weather. According to Isidore, wind trapped in a cloud will tear it violently as it seeks an outlet, resulting in thunder. Bede ventured into the realms of prediction: 'if the sky is red at night, it means good weather; if it is red in the morning, it means bad weather.' Aristotle's *Meteorologica*, long forgotten in Europe, was translated into Arabic, then reintroduced into the West in the thirteenth century, first through a Latin translation from Arabic, then through another from Greek. Among the scholars of the thirteenth and fourteenth centuries, Albert le Grand and Jean Buridan adopted Aristotle's system and attempted to refine and complete it. Despite its naïveties, this quest for natural causes prefigured modern meteorology. It was a fundamentally scientific approach (at least in intention), an attempt to separate the natural from the supernatural.

In fact, the natural and the supernatural complemented rather than opposed one another. Like the whole of creation, the laws of nature were thought to be the work of God. The people of the Middle Ages tried to navigate more or less coherently between Earth and Heaven. Their attempts at rational interpretation could not eradicate the respect, fear and helplessness induced by uncontrollable and generally unpredictable phenomena. All these manifestations may have had a natural dimension, but they seemed to express something that was more essential to human destiny.

God was still the master and continued to transmit his messages to mankind. But the Devil was involved as well. The belief that the air harboured demons was already widespread in antiquity and was especially favoured by Plato and his disciples. St Augustine's *The City of God* incorporates this idea into a Christian context: God banished the rebel angels to the lower regions of the air.[4] Thomas Aquinas also took the airborne nature of demons into consideration. The existence of creatures who delighted in tormenting humans could explain the vagaries of the weather: 'Atmospheric disturbances and the permanent conflicts of water and wind were thus the sign of demonic life, as opposed to the serenity of the skies. They prevented souls from ascending to heaven and hovered above the Earth, intent upon the destruction of human beings.'[5]

The rigours of the climate could be explained in three different but complementary ways: God was punishing men, Satan was persecuting them, or, in a dialectical synthesis, both were involved – atmospheric disturbances were manifestations of the eternal struggle between God and the Devil, between Good and Evil. In such circumstances it was hard to decide what course to take when calamity struck – should one invoke God or curse the Devil? But these transcendental interpretations did not exclude the search for natural explanations. Meteorology was torn between science and religion.

The meteorological records that have come down to us from the Middle Ages (of some use to climate historians if treated with caution, as we have seen) focus on the unusual. Nobody thought in terms of 'averages' or data gathered over a period of time. Meteorology was a collection of isolated and preferably dramatic events. This attitude still prevails today; records and norms are left to the experts, while the general public remains obsessed with climatic excesses. Nothing has changed apart from the conditions of perception: the people of the Middle Ages experienced climatic excesses in a specific mental and material context. On one hand, they displayed a certain fatalism and a capacity, probably greater than our own, to integrate disasters into the natural order of things. On the other, it could not be denied that the weather was capable of delivering devastating shocks. The essentially rural civilization of the time was highly sensitive to atmospheric variations; technology was rudimentary and, for populations living at subsistence level, any disturbance was likely to cause a catastrophe. Moreover, God, the Devil or both together were the origin of climatic excess; mankind naturally wondered what kind of fate lay in store for it. But if we anticipate a little the concerns of today, these distinctions do not seem enough to suggest a clear contrast between medieval attitudes and those of our own era. Technological civilization is also partly dependent on climate, and our own catastrophe scenarios (as well as the price that may have to be paid for human error) are as dramatic as medieval analogues, although God and the Devil seem to have dropped out of the meteorological business.

When we read medieval texts, we are confronted with an impressive parade of devastating storms, torrential rains, floods, severe droughts, abundant snowfalls and excessively cold winters. We come across syntheses such as the one noted by a monk: 'the year of grace 1219, the year of the nocturnal flood and of Seigneur Honorius, Pope'. The excesses of the weather were usually symbolically linked to historical facts or interpreted as omens. Meteorological or cosmic disturbances sometimes herald or accompany wars. Sometimes they are the prelude to the death of a famous person. On the eve of Charlemagne's death, the universe seemed to have descended into chaos: solar and lunar eclipses were accompanied by earth tremors and the basilica at Aachen was struck by lightning. The death of Stephen the Great

(1457–1504), the most famous of the princes of Moldavia, was preceded by an extremely cold winter and followed by heavy rain and floods.[6] Other consequences – droughts or excessive rainfall, poor harvests, famines and epidemics – were not purely symbolic but part of a genuine chain of events.

1033: *the testimony of Rodulfus Glaber*

The catalogue of highly dramatized and portent-laden bad weather includes an account as worthy of inclusion in any apocalyptic anthology as the biblical story of the Flood or the present-day dossier on global warming. It is the work of Rodulfus Glaber, a Burgundian monk, and it appears in his mid-eleventh-century *The Five Books of the Histories*, which chronicles the period from 900 to 1044. The following extracts are taken from Glaber's description of the famine that ravaged Burgundy in 1033.

Some time later a famine began to ravage the whole earth, and death threatened almost all the human race. The weather was so unseasonable that no season was suitable for the sowing of any crop, and floods prevented the gathering in of the harvest. It seemed as though the elements were warring amongst themselves, but for certain they were wreaking vengeance upon human presumption. Rain fell so continuously everywhere that for three years furrows for seed could not be properly driven . . . This avenging famine began in the Orient, and after devastating Greece passed to Italy and thence to Gaul and the whole English people . . .

After men had eaten beasts and birds, under the pressure of rampant famine they began to eat carrion and things too horrible to mention. Some tried to escape death by eating the roots of the forest and the herbs of the stream, but in vain, for there is no escape from the wrath of the vengeance of God except to God himself. It is terrible to relate the evils which then befell mankind. Alas, a thing formerly little heard of happened: ravening hunger drove men to devour human flesh! Travellers were set upon by men stronger than themselves, and their dismembered flesh was cooked over fires and eaten. Many who had fled from place to place from the famine, when they found shelter at last, were slaughtered in the night as food for those who had welcomed them. Many showed an apple or an egg to children, then dragged them to out-of-the-way places and killed and ate them. In many places the bodies of the dead were dragged from the earth, also to appease hunger. This raging madness rose to such proportions that solitary beasts were less likely to be attacked by brigands than men. The custom of eating human flesh had grown so common that one fellow sold it ready cooked in the market-place of Tournus like that of some beast. When he was arrested he did not deny the shameful charge. He was bound and burned to death . . .

Some three miles from the city of Mâcon there is a church dedicated to St John; a lonely place, it is set in the forest of Châtenet. Nearby a wild man had built his hut, who preyed upon those passing by or calling at his hut, killing them for to serve for his unspeakable meals. One day a man and his wife called there and took a short rest. Looking around the corners of the hut the man observed the severed heads of men, women, and children. Instantly he paled and tried to leave, but the evil owner of the hut tried to make him stay. However, fearful of this fatal trap, he prevailed and fled with his wife to the city. Arriving there he told what he had seen to Count Otto and other citizens. They sent a band of men to ascertain the truth; hastening thither, they found the cruel fellow in his hut, together with forty-eight severed heads whose bodies he had devoured with his beastly mouth. They took him to the city, tied him to a post in a barn, and, as we ourselves later saw, burnt him to death . . .

Faces were pale and emaciated and the skin of many appeared inflated with air; men's very voices, reduced to extreme thinness, piped like those of dying birds. None the less, wolves gorged themselves at that time on the corpses of the dead – which lay all around, too many to be buried – after a long interval once more preying on men . . .

In order to punish the sins of men this terrible pestilence raged throughout the whole world for three years . . . It was believed that the order of the seasons and the elements, which had ruled all past ages from the beginning, had fallen into perpetual chaos, and with it had come the end of mankind. But what was more astounding than anything else was that it was very rare indeed for anyone, under the impact of this secret and divine vengeance, to raise his heart and hands unto the Lord as he should have done, with a contrite heart and humble body begging for His aid.[7]

It is not our purpose to question the veracity of this narrative. Rodulfus Glaber selects his material with great skill; his scene-setting is adroit and his sense of drama is perfect. However, it is his message that concerns us. It articulates some of the elements that have so often characterized this type of human and cosmic crisis since the dawn of civilization. Human beings are flawed and, worse still, incapable of repentance because they cannot grasp the magnitude of their flaws. Climatic disturbances act as divine punishments and their consequences are far-reaching. It is not simply a matter of famine but of an abrupt collapse of civilization, a kind of dehumanization. Moreover, our monk refers explicitly to a possible extinction of the human species, although such remarks should be placed in their proper perspective. Glaber's *The Five Books of the Histories* is divided between the accomplishments and sufferings of the age and between its hopes and fears. It testifies not only to the precarious nature of human existence, but also to the dawn of the West's renewal, a prelude, therefore, to its ascendancy. The episode of 1033 should be read as a warning. If we seek a definitive, or almost definitive, end of the world, we have to go back to the time of the Flood.

NOAH

The Flood is the meteorological disaster par excellence.[8] We are familiar with its Judaeo-Christian version: Noah, warned by God of his decision to destroy corrupt humanity, constructed an ark (150 metres long, 50 metres wide and 15 metres high) to accommodate his family and a pair of every animal on earth. Rain fell for forty days, inundating the world and rising to a height of to 7.5 metres above the tops of the highest mountains. The water gradually diminished over the course of 150 days, leaving the vessel stranded on Mount Ararat, in what is now Armenia. The descendants of Noah's three sons, Shem, Ham and Japheth, repopulated the Earth.

The belief that the Flood was an exclusively biblical event persisted for centuries. It was therefore a surprise when, in 1872, cuneiform tablets from the library of Assurbanipal of Nineveh were found to contain a narrative very similar to the story of the Judaeo-Christian Flood. The tablets formed the eleventh song of the Babylonian *Epic of Gilgamesh*, a text that pre-dated the Bible. Subsequently, an even earlier Babylonian text, *Atrahasis* or *Poem of the Supersage* (c.1700 BC) was unearthed. This is the first written account of the Flood. At around 1300 BC, a modified and expanded text had been incorporated into the *Epic of Gilgamesh*. A new version, heavily revised but still closely linked with its predecessors, was eventually inserted into the Bible.

The Babylonian Noah, called Atrahasis and later Utnapishtim, built a curious and even more richly symbolic vessel than the one described in the Bible. It resembled a cube, a kind of sixty metre-long floating box, and each of its seven decks was divided into nine compartments, a structure that mirrored the Mesopotamian concept of the universe. The parable is easy to interpret: the vessel is a microcosm, the seed of a new world designed to survive the destruction of the old. The Mesopotamian origin of the Biblical Flood is no longer in doubt, although the conclusions that may be drawn from it are inevitably contradictory. Some see it as confirmation of the narrative's truth and 'universality', while others regard it as nothing more than the passage of a legendary motif from one culture to another.

For many centuries both Christians and Jews accepted the literal truth of the Flood. With the emergence of modern science and the dominance of reason, things became more complicated. Three attitudes resulted from this. The first, acceptance of the traditional version, persists to this day; many people continue to believe in the Biblical version of the Flood. The second was negation. For Voltaire – who exemplified the devotion to Reason – the Bible was simply a compendium of nonsense and its Flood could be dismissed with a joke: 'I do not understand how God created a race only to drown it and replace it with an even more wicked race.'[9] The third attitude was more complex. It attempted to translate the biblical narrative into scientific language and thus highlight the role of cosmic or natural agents. Such interpretations could either support the idea of divine intervention or they could replace it and cancel it out.[10]

In 1681 Thomas Burnet published *Telluris Theoria Sacra* (*The Sacred Theory of the Earth*), a highly accomplished synthesis of the

Bible and science that affords equal weight to each authority. If the word of God is true, science can only confirm it. At the beginning, paradisaical conditions prevailed on Earth, a fact justified by astronomy; since the planet always maintained the same distance from the sun, the climate was consistently mild. But the incessant bombardment of the sun's rays caused much of the water that lay underground to evaporate, exerting pressure on the Earth's crust, which eventually burst and released the water, hence the Flood. Physical causes will also announce the end of the world; a terrible drought will be followed by an all-consuming 'Flood' of fire. The Earth will be divided into two parts, one liquid and the other composed of vapours. The latter will soar into space and form a new heaven and a new Earth. The Book of Revelation had predicted these events and science, it appears, can confirm them.

This combination of biblical and scientific speculation enjoyed a prolonged vogue, especially in England. The emerging science of geology made a significant contribution to the debate as it seemed to confirm everything the Bible said. Some years after Burnet, John Woodward inserted the Flood into the natural history of the planet (*Essay Towards the Natural History of the Earth*, 1695). In 1696, mathematician William Whiston took cosmic interpretation even further in his *New Theory of the Earth*. He attributed the Flood to the trajectory of a comet, which would one day bring about the end of the world. Even after 1800, diluvial geology continued its career unperturbed. It was represented at Oxford by William Buckland, a professor of geology. His *Reliquiae Diluvianae*, or *Observations on Geological Phenomena, Attesting the Action of an Universal Deluge* (1823–4), treated the biblical Flood as the last great catastrophe in the history of the Earth.

The English scholars mentioned above were reluctant to break with God. But this kind of divorce, though still not widely practised, was more acceptable in the land of Voltaire. The French could retain the Flood and jettison the divinity without too much formality. The model of a Flood without God was comprehensively outlined by Nicolas-Antoine Boulanger (1722–1759) in his post-humously published *L'Antiquité dévoilée par ses ouvrages* (1766). The causes of the cataclysm were not obvious but had to be sought in nature: 'In an instant, all the seas were thrown over our continents, and nations were destroyed in the blink of an eye.' Earth tremors and the planet's central fire put the finishing touches to the disaster. This fire 'emerged from the ground; a frightful noise announced its activity; mountains and plains burst into flames. In a thousand places, blazing volcanoes spewed water and fire, burning rivers and torrents of lava that consumed what the waters had respected.'[11] It is almost like an eyewitness account.

The most serious aspect of the Flood, according to Boulanger, was its destruction of an evolved civilization (perhaps even more evolved than our own). The rejection of the Bible meant that human life acquired a far longer history than the several generations that had separated the Creation from the Flood.

> The Flood, which was the tomb of so many nations, was also the tomb of reason and philosophy, the tomb of the arts, sciences and laws. It took many happy and peaceful centuries to repair the damage… Modern societies draw all their origins from the small number of unfortunates who had the sad advantage of surviving the old human race and the great changes that occurred in nature.[12]

We are the survivors – still fearful, still confused – of an end of the world. This explains the superstitious and religious character of the 'new man', an apparently less accomplished specimen than his ancestor. This confused being has deified the blind forces of nature. It was not God who sent the Flood. It was the Flood that caused man to invent God. To dismiss the Bible almost entirely and to retain only the Flood is an approach that I will later attempt to include in a long series of historical interpretations.

According to Georges Cuvier's *Discours sur les révolutions de la surface du globe* (1821), the Flood has a tendency to propagate itself:

> Life on this earth has often been troubled by terrible events. Human beings without number have fallen victim to these catastrophes. Some, living on dry land, have been swallowed up by floods. Others, living in the midst of the waters, have been stranded as the sea bed has risen to the surface.[13]

Boucher de Perthes, one of the founders of the discipline of pre-history and author of *Antiquités celtiques et antédiluviennes* (1846–64) claimed that the human race had existed since time immemorial and had been subject to periodic disasters, the biblical Flood being the most recent. 'The human species, like animal species, has been renewed more than once, not in totality but for the greater part.'[14] De Perthes believed that we would discover traces of civilizations that had existed long before the Flood.

Louis Figuier, one of the great nineteenth-century popularizers of science, preferred the biblical narrative. In *La Terre avant le Déluge* (1863), he divided the Quaternary into three distinct periods: 1) The European floods (which had occurred before the appearance of man and had resulted from the formation of the mountain ranges). 2) The glacial era, still prior to man. 3) The creation of man and the Asian Flood. Traditional interpretations of the Bible are therefore correct: man is 'recent'. The biblical Flood had indeed occurred, although confined to a part of Asia, the only region known to humanity at that time. The cause of the phenomenon is quite clear to Figuier: 'All the particularities of the biblical account can be explained by the volcanic eruption and the rain of mud that preceded the formation of Mount Ararat. The waters that inundated these countries came from a volcanic eruption accompanied by massive clouds of steam . . .'[15] The fact is that the biblical Flood remained firmly in its place in universal histories and scholarly manuals until the middle of the nineteenth century and even beyond.[16] Subsequently, given the growth of geological and prehistorical studies, its defenders were forced to restrict its scope and to acknowledge that the history of humanity was much longer than tradition allowed for.

Advocates of the historicity of the Flood naturally focused on the regions of the near and Middle East, particularly Mesopotamia, where the narrative had originated. In 1885, Eduard Suess (1831–1914), a celebrated Austrian geologist, published the first volume of *Das Antlitz der Erde*, one of the most important geological syntheses of its time. Remarkably, the first chapter is dedicated to the Flood. According to Suess, it had been caused by an earthquake in the Persian Gulf, followed by a gigantic 'tsunami' or sea wave.[17] Another explanation takes into account the 'local' flooding that periodically affected Mesopotamia. The British archaeologist C. Leonard Woolley (1880–1960) strongly supported the historicity of a Mesopotamian flood: although it had been somewhat exaggerated by legendary tradition, its traces were visible and it had had a considerable effect on the life of the region.[18] Consideration was also given to the ice thaw that followed the last glacial period.[19] More recently, in 1997, the American geologist William Ryan has suggested that a geological upheaval occurring some 7,500 years ago may have forced the waters of the Mediterranean into the Black Sea, an irruption that would have flooded inhabited areas. However, none of these interpretations is very convincing. The earthquake imagined by Suess is simple supposition; the Mesopotamian inundations are also disputed; the melting of prehistoric ice was a gradual phenomenon and could not have caused a sudden and massive invasion of water. As for the Black Sea, research continues.

Difficulties of interpretation do not prevent believers believing. Several expeditions have scaled Mount Ararat (5,165 metres) in search of the debris of the Ark. The astronaut John Irving participated in one of them. But the most assiduous 'Ark hunter' was the Frenchman Fernand Navarre who, in the early 1950s, brought back pieces of wood that might have come from the biblical vessel. It is not hard to understand why the quest continues: Noah symbolizes the critical moment in Christian (or Judaeo-Christian) world history. Like Adam and Eve before him and later, Jesus, he is found at the origin of the western civilization that has since conquered the planet.

FLOODS AND ENDS OF THE WORLD: *an interpretation*

The Mesopotamian-Judaic Flood is just one version of an almost universal myth. The Greeks had the Deucalian flood. After the waters retreated Deucalion and his wife Pyrrha recreated humanity by the singular method of casting stones behind them: the stones thrown by Deucalion metamorphosed into men while those thrown by Pyrrha turned into women.

India too has produced several variants of the Flood myth. China has a less fatalistic version according to which men raised dams, dug canals and finally forced the waters to withdraw. In fact, few regions of the world seem to have escaped this terrible inundation; apart from sub-Saharan Africa and Japan, we find it almost everywhere. The myth is particularly strong among the Indian tribes of the American continent. The first missionaries to arrive in the New World approved of these diluvial stories, seeing them as further proof of the historicity of the universal Flood. The myths could also support secular interpretations. Boulanger, for example, took their universality and concordance as proof that the cataclysm had actually occurred.

The Flood, therefore, has greater ramifications than the likelihood of Mesopotamian inundations or other disasters that affected a relatively small region. On the other hand, the quasi-universality of the belief (expressed through widely differentiated accounts) does not necessarily provide convincing proof of the existence of a worldwide flood. The idea of a universal Flood (or at least a deluge that affected the inhabited world at a particular time) can be advanced in religious terms, but when examined in the light of science and reason, it is difficult to believe in it. Yet the tradition is universal. How can this contradiction be resolved?

The theory of a localized inundation that was transformed into the Flood of legend probably contains an element of truth. Such catastrophic events have happened and continue to happen all over the world. For a tribe, the world does not extend much beyond its own territory. The 'universalization' of local events is entirely understandable in a primitive era. We only have to read the Bible to see how it works: the 'external' world hardly existed for the Jews. The entire course of history unfolded in Palestine. But the real inundations are simply the 'primary materials' of the Flood myth. Its logic is different and its meaning lies elsewhere. Water is just one of several agents; fire often plays a supporting role. While it is easy to explain the Flood through less extensive inundations, a global conflagration cannot be explained by forest fires.

The Aztecs, who believed the world had already been destroyed three or four times, could draw on an impressive climatic repertoire that included drought, fire, hurricanes and floods. They predicted that one of these agents would bring about yet another end of the world. Besides inventing the Flood – or at least its most influential version – the Babylonians devised a more general theory of global destruction. Their astronomers worked out that the alignment of all the planets (a return to their original position) marked the end of a 'great year' or cosmic era. This represented the end of a cycle and each time it occurred the world would perish by water and by fire.

The Greek philosopher Heraclitus (c.540–480 BC) supported destruction by fire at the end of each cycle. The Stoics developed his idea, attributing the periodic combustion of the world to a universal conflagration. Other philosophical schools thought in similar terms. Polybius, a historian of the second century BC, thought the history of mankind had been and would continue to be punctuated by disasters such as inundations, epidemics and famines; mankind is decimated and civilizations collapse each time one of these catastrophes occurs.[20] In *De Natura Rerum*, the Latin poet and epicurean philosopher Lucretius (c.98–55 BC) argued for the 'objective' necessity of periodic disasters: the world had already succumbed twice, by fire and water, and the future looked gloomy – the earth and sky would come to their end.[21] A century later, the philosopher Seneca (4 BC–AD 65) imagined 'the last day of mankind' in his *Quaestiones Naturales*: water would emerge from everywhere, inundating and literally dissolving the land.[22]

But floods and other natural disasters are less important than the mentality that combines such events, exaggerates them and invests them with a higher meaning: the belief, in some way elementary, that everything must one day collapse. History was first imagined as a resolutely cyclical process. The analogy with cosmic and natural cycles – the succession of day and night, the phases of the moon, the alternating seasons – is obvious. But the cyclical view also corresponds with the precarious nature of the historical process – the constant succession of rises and falls, natural disasters and invasions. Imagined history is thus punctuated by instances of the end of the world, although these are usually incomplete. There are always a few survivors – as in the aftermath of the Flood – to ensure that humanity returns to the path of history.

Religious interpretations of floods were based on the arbitrary will – or simply the whims – of the gods. Philosophical interpretations reveal the implacable mechanics of the universe. However, if we compare the biblical deluge with the Mesopotamian model, we see that the former is a case apart. While the latter was simply a gratuitous game of the gods and had no particular ethical meaning, the one God of the Hebrews had a high conception of his responsibility and of the destiny of his people. The distinction between Good and Evil became clear. Humanity had to be punished for its sins but was given the opportunity to start again. The Flood anticipates the Last Judgement, the definitive end, the point at which the chosen and the damned would be locked into their condition for eternity. The function of the Flood is therefore to endow men with a sense of responsibility; they are forced to learn that they will pay dearly for their sins.

This ethical conception of human destiny departs from traditional cyclical history (although, like the Flood itself, it incorporates certain elements of finality and renewal). Cycles led nowhere; if history chased its tail, it offered no possibility for the development of a higher purpose or a project of spiritual perfection. The history of the Jews, on the other hand, was distinguished by its linearity and motivation. It would not be repeated and it involved a greater element of human responsibility. This schema would be adopted by Christianity and enlarged to fit the scale of the world. It was the first coherent and global version of progress, a process of spiritual perfection that would end by fusing the City of Man with the City of God.

'Ends of the world' provide us with a sensitive barometer of the march of history. Their intensity is proportional to history's dynamic. For a completely static society (a theoretical model), the 'end' would have little meaning. However, an acceleration of historical processes entails an accumulation of factors – malfunctions, breakdowns, fear of the unknown, social disintegration, greater deracination or marginalization – that stimulate the apocalyptic imagination. A history that moves too fast effaces landmarks and induces vertigo. This was notably the case in Mesopotamia and the Near East, where the apocalyptic imagination was moulded by the endless succession of rises and falls of cities and empires. Another conflictive process was unleashed by the passage from the Greek city to the Greco-Roman world. The scale of history had begun to change; it was shifting from urban community to empire, from a limited and fortified space to a vast and all-consuming space. Social crises, particularly the ruination of the peasantry, exacerbated the malaise. The Roman Empire was overextended and could not function effectively (in spatiotemporal terms, it was far more extensive than the world we know today). Apocalyptic scenarios proliferated, their function being to put an end to a corrupt and unjust world. This generalized state of discontent and anxiety facilitated the expansion and triumph of Christianity. The doctrine of salvation and of a history endowed with meaning, which lay at the heart of its message, clashed completely with the drift of the Roman world and a history that led either nowhere or to yet more turbulence and injustice.[23]

Christian theology put emphasis on the idea that the world would come to an end; indeed, it was the very goal of human history. However, the Revelation of St John, an obscure and infinitely interpretable text, posited a double end. First, the second coming of the Messiah would signal the initiation of a thousand-year-long earthly kingdom and the effective termination of history.

This hypothesis forms the basis of the millenarian ideologies and movements that claimed that humanity could enjoy justice and happiness in this world before taking full advantage of it in the next. The thousand years of happiness would be followed by the Last Judgment and the definitive end of time. Both ends would be preceded by various signs and accompanied by cosmic and human upheavals. The greatest difficulty, therefore, lay in deciphering history: how were the signs to be interpreted and what position did misfortunes and disturbances occupy on the apocalyptic scale? For example, did the sacking of Rome by Alaric and the Visigoths in AD 410 prefigure the end of the world? Apparently, many people thought it did. Bede recounts that, about AD 600, Pope Gregory the Great provided the English king Ethelbert, a recent convert to Christianity, with a list of the omens that would announce the end of time: 'changes in the sky and terrors from the heavens; unseasonable tempests; wars, famine, pestilence and earthquakes in divers places' – every imaginable disaster, in fact.[24]

The dynamic of the West has been stimulating and exaggerating end-of-the-world and end-of-civilization scenarios for over a thousand years. The accelerating march of history has engendered far greater hopes and fears than those aroused by the slow development of traditional civilizations. Social structures have undergone increasingly rapid and radical transformations, a process which shows no sign of slowing down. Each generation has had to accustom itself to living in a permanent state of crisis. The world is increasingly open, diverse and more prone to conflict. This fascinating and daunting evolution has been responsible for a wide variety of scenarios. Since 1516, the year in which Thomas More's *Utopia* appeared, the West has continued to produce an impressive quantity of utopian writings, technological schemes, social projects and projections and fictions concerning the near or distant future. This mixture of contradictory projects reflects in equal measure a growing confidence in human ability and the fear that our frenetic course will end badly. No other civilization has ever combined such a high degree of optimism and pessimism.

The period between the twelfth and seventeenth centuries (from the end of the Middle Ages to the birth of the modern era) was responsible for a dazzling array of end-of-the-world scenarios and millenarian projects. They may be viewed as the reaction of a society that had emerged from the Middle Ages with a relative degree of stability, only to find itself entering a disturbing period of change. A large number of people from all social classes had been uprooted and were dreaming of radical change, either in the form of the Last Judgment or, preferably, the Messianic kingdom. Moreover, as wars, religious conflicts, epidemics and other disasters could be read as apocalyptic omens, they exacerbated an already generalized sense of anxiety. Luther was convinced that the world would end in one hundred years' time, perhaps even earlier. Columbus situated the event more precisely, in 1656. This highly charged atmosphere of expectancy sometimes led to the kind of hysteria typified by witch hunts: humanity was threatened by a thousand hidden dangers and the battle between Good and Evil had reached a paroxysm.[25] The vertiginous effects of historical acceleration are not easy to bear.

THE FLOOD IN THE MODERN ERA

Let us return to the Flood, an inevitable item in any catalogue of portents and calamities. The German mathematician and astrologer Johann Stöffler announced that another universal flood would occur in 1524 (Germany at this time was already sinking into religious and social conflict). According to Pierre Bayle's perhaps exaggerated account, Stöffler's warning was taken seriously: 'The terror had gone beyond the people to the princes, and even to the *savants* . . . those who had houses near the sea or rivers had abandoned them or sold their land and furniture at huge losses . . . In France, the terror was so great that many people thought they were losing their minds.'[26] As the age had a solid biblical culture its people knew how to deal with floods. Some began to construct arks; Auriol, president of the Toulouse *parlement*, was one of these new Noahs.

The year 1524 was not marked by excessive rainfall. Astrologers adjusted their forecasts but did not give way on the main point: 'The facts have since demonstrated that the constellations had in reality announced misfortunes without number: miseries, anguish and troubles followed by bloody carnage.' Jean Bodin, the illustrious political theorist and devotee of astrology, reopened the historical and astrological dossier for 1524 in his treatise *De la République*, which contained a long list of conflicts and massacres, including a Turkish victory over Christian forces and 'a strange outpouring of water . . . great storms and floods in many countries'. Not the Flood in all its splendour, perhaps, but at least a little foretaste, characteristically combined with various other misfortunes.[27]

As time went on, the religious interpretations of our world gave way to science. The Enlightenment triggered a massive anti-mythology operation. But the result was less the demolition of ancient schemas than their translation into scientific and philosophical language. In comparison with previous centuries, however, there was greater optimism and confidence in the future; the modern idea of progress had begun to take its first steps. But a certain feeling of precariousness remained. God may have seemed less threatening (especially for those who no longer believed in him), but uncontrollable cosmic forces were ready to carry on his work. The West was shocked by the devastating effects of the Lisbon earthquake of 1755; Voltaire treated it at length. But the

thinkers of the time, like Whiston before them, were more fascinated by comets.

In *Lettre sur la comète* (1742), Maupertuis, a French mathematician and president of the Berlin Academy, presents an impressive
list of the effects a collision with this celestial object could produce. Apart from the shock itself, which would shatter the Earth,
the approach of a comet might cause dramatic changes through
the power of universal attraction. The Earth's axis might be
altered to such an extent that the equator would shift towards
the poles and the poles towards the equator. It is not hard to see
what effect this would have on climate. Worse might follow if the
Earth's orbit around the sun was altered: our planet would become
a kind of comet itself and would be exposed to the greatest vicis-
situdes: 'sometimes burned in its perihelion, sometimes frozen
by the cold of the most distant regions of the heavens'.[28] This is a
new way of interpreting climatic deviations; it integrates them
into the great universal mechanism governed by Newton's laws.

The French scholar Laplace describes the consequences of a
cosmic encounter in his *Exposition du système du monde* (1796):

> The axis and movement of rotation changed; the seas aban-
> doning their ancient position to rush to the new equator; most
> men and animals drowned in this universal flood or were
> destroyed by the violent shock to the planet; entire species
> wiped out; every monument to human industry overturned.
> Such are the disasters that the shock of a comet must produce
> should its mass be comparable to that of the Earth.[29]

Boulanger had noted the possibility of physical causes but
Laplace's scientific argument goes much further. Comets had
caused the Flood, or floods, in the past and would probably do
so again.

By the nineteenth century, progress (assisted by the evolutionist perspective) had become the governing principle of western civilization. For many centuries, the Biblical narrative and its exegetes had restricted past history to a span of a few thousand years and future time to a probably even briefer episode. The eighteenth century had opened the first breach in this system. By the following century, the long-duration theory had effectively replaced the biblical version: human history stretched back farther than had been believed, and would continue into a very distant future. Like any era, the nineteenth century had its share of pessimists, particularly among those who had already glimpsed the dangers of technology. But the optimists were more numerous and more vocal. In short, it was the most optimistic period in history, the one most confident in the perfectibility of the future.

From time to time, disasters were announced or imagined. The possibility of another Flood was not discounted but it did not present an immediate threat. The French mathematician Alphonse-Joseph Adhémar developed a physical and mathematical theory of the periodicity of floods in *Les Révolutions de la mer* (1842). According to Adhémar, fluctuating temperatures caused ice to accumulate and then disintegrate at both poles. This produced periodic changes in the planet's centre of gravity and each shift caused a universal flood. The last disaster, at the North Pole, had happened 4,200 years ago, and the next, at the South Pole, would occur in 6,300 years time. At least humanity had plenty of time to get used to the idea!

The sociologist Gabriel Tarde opted for a shorter time span. His *Fragment d'histoire future*, written in 1884 but not published until 1896, predicts a 'débâcle' in 2489, due to a sudden reduction in the sun's energy: 'The entire population of Norway, northern Russia and Siberia will freeze to death overnight.' Humanity initially takes refuge in Arabia and the Sahara but the intensifying cold soon renders the entire surface of the planet uninhabitable. The survivors are forced to descend into the bowels of the earth. Six centuries after the cataclysm, 50 million people are living in underground cities and existing on frozen animal carcasses.[30]

The production of catastrophe scenarios continued but, for a while at least, they were distinguished by their moderation. According to the dominant theory, the world would succumb to old age rather than to accident. Camille Flammarion (a veritable scientific 'institution' in his day) synthesized the different theories in *La Fin du monde* (1894). In the twenty-fifth century, a comet or an asteroid smashes into the earth; it causes millions of deaths and massive destruction but civilization survives. No catastrophe can halt the march of progress. Humanity will survive for another ten million years, until the planet is worn out. Flammarion offers several possible explanations for the degradation of the physical world. Erosion, for example: in a few million years the earth's surface will be completely flat, and covered by the sea. If the sea still exists, that is, for another scenario focuses on the drying-up of the planet, as on the moon or Mars. It was thought at the time that the planets illustrated Earth's past and future; as Mars was older than Earth, it indicated our prospects. Water will gradually give way to soil, a process exacerbated by chemical action. At the same time, the atmosphere will become more rarefied (in accordance with Martian and lunar models) and will progressively lose its water vapour, which has the property of retaining heat. Earth will become increasingly cold. So in 10 million years' time the Earth will have a completely flat surface, dried up seas, a rarefied atmosphere and an arctic climate. Humanity will revert to barbarity before dying out completely. The human species will die of cold, the fate probably suffered by the Martians. It is interesting to note that after millions of years of progress, climate retains its sovereignty. Man can find no way of preventing the deterioration of physical conditions nor of leaving the planet and settling elsewhere. The nineteenth-century imagination had its limits; the twentieth century would exceed them.

1900: *concatenation of disasters*

We have now arrived at the turn of the century, a significant landmark for the logic of the imagination and particularly for its penchant for disaster scenarios. 1900 marks the point at which the imbalances and potential dangers engendered by the acceleration of progress begin to acquire clearer definition and arouse a wave of anxiety. These concerns are not entirely new; technology has always had its share of sceptics and enemies. However, the picture now darkens dramatically. The utopian promise of a radiant future loses ground to the anti-utopian vision of a dehumanizing one. Artists, quicker to react or perhaps just more sensitive, staged their own 'end of the world' by rejecting classical models and inventing cubism, futurism, abstract art and other novel forms of expression. In 1918, Oswald Spengler achieved great success with a book explicitly titled *The Decline of the West*. Cyclical history was back in fashion, while the still powerful idea of progress took on an undertone of decadence. World wars, bloody revolutions, totalitarian regimes and serial genocide seemed to confirm the aura of disenchantment.

Just as cosmic signs customarily accompany or anticipate human disasters, nature also began to impose its presence in a particularly vehement way. In 1883, the Indonesian island of Krakatoa had been devastated by a tremendous volcanic eruption that killed at least 40,000 people. In 1902, Mount Pelée, on the Caribbean island of Martinique, erupted, emitting a lava cloud that claimed 30,000 victims in the town of Saint-Pierre. In 1906, extraordinarily violent earthquakes destroyed part of San Francisco and two Chilean cities,

Valparaiso and Santiago. Europe's turn came in 1908, with the terrible Messina earthquake; the death toll was put at 100,000 but may have been even higher. There was also some impressive flooding. In January 1910, the Seine rose 8.5 metres in Paris. Part of the great city was literally submerged, a striking rehearsal for the next Flood! 1910 was also the year of Halley's comet. Astronomers had calculated an encounter; in fact they were simply predicting that the planet would pass through the comet's tail, whose particles were thought to be too fine to penetrate Earth's dense atmosphere. Yet the situation gave rise to a genuine panic; people were especially afraid that the atmosphere would be contaminated by cyanogen, the toxic gas supposedly carried in the comet's tail. But nothing happened, nothing at all. The comet merely activated a widespread neurosis that was ready to respond to any unusual occurrence.

Moreover, as anxiety increased the dangers were more or less interchangeable. The 'other' assumed a more threatening aspect. European nations began to fear each other. Even worse was the 'yellow peril' arising in the Far East. The imminent conquest of Europe by a Sino-Japanese coalition was already being announced in some quarters; the Flood had acquired an equally frightening variant in the form of a 'human tide'.

We can already see the outlines of a model. The most diverse events – political, geological, climatic and cosmic – were exaggerated and grouped together for reasons that owed much more to an increasingly negative state of mind than to the objective importance of the phenomena themselves. Natural phenomena were mediated through the essentially conflictive discourses of society, ideology and politics. When the social atmosphere is under strain, nature also seems more restless than usual. As soon as we begin to imagine the collapse of civilization, we find that nature is ready and willing to lend assistance. Some of its effects (like the earthquakes above) were indeed spectacular, but the way in which they were integrated into an interpretive system was simply a manifestation of the socio-ideological tensions of the time; these quite logically resulted in wars and revolutions, rather than in the destruction of the world by fire or water.

It is instructive to observe how some scientists and popularizers of science became caught up in this system. In 1905, the French geophysicist Alphonse Berget declared: 'The bursting of the earth's crust, which is relatively thin, is a constant possibility . . . We are dancing on a volcano . . . Given the thinness of the crust that supports us, it is astonishing that it is still intact.'[31] In 1909, Flammarion went one better (in the process contradicting his own optimistic schema in *La Fin du monde*): 'This planet is still not definitively constituted . . . The human race arrived too early and settled down prematurely.'[32] The astronomer and popular science writer Théophile Moreux threatened humanity with a series of collapses of the earth's crust in *Les Tremblements de terre* (1909). Much of Europe would be submerged; Russia would be wiped out; France would be reduced to a few islands and Great Britain to Scotland and a corner of Ireland. The earthquakes of the early 1900s had certainly stimulated the imagination.

There was a resurgence of interest in the 'lost' continent of Atlantis, which did not seem to provide a very reassuring example. If entire continents had been swallowed up over the course of the Earth's geological history, there was no reason to believe that the same geological forces would not act in a similar way in the near future. In 1905 *Je sais tout* magazine published an article by Flammarion, which described a possible invasion by the sea. In an effort to make the scenario more convincing, it was accompanied by a very realistic drawing by Henri Lanos entitled *Le Déluge de Paris. L'Opéra au fond de la mer*.[33] Tourists of the future wishing to sample the delights of the City of Light would have to get there by submarine. The floods of 1910 seemed to confirm this aquatic vision, partially at least.

The English scientist Leon Lewis published a commentary on the likelihood of another flood entitled *The Great Glacial Deluge and its Impending Recurrence*. The Antarctic ice seemed to be on the verge of breaking up; if it did so, sea levels would rise and sea temperatures would drop. Ocean currents would carry icebergs to the coasts of Europe; most of the continent would be submerged and almost all organic life destroyed. It might not happen tomorrow but it was a distinct possibility. The January 1902 issue of the *Journal des voyages* published an article on Lewis's thesis, accompanied by an edifying image of the Eiffel Tower collapsing under masses of ice.[34]

The 'cosmic agency formula' continued to exert its influence. H. G. Wells's story *The Star* (1897) contains a detailed and apparently rigorous analysis of what would happen if an alien star burst into our solar system (in fact he was simply revamping the old story of the comet). Again, we are offered the familiar succession of rising temperatures, floods, gigantic tidal waves, earthquakes and the collapse of the earth's crust.

The 1907 edition of the highly popular *Almanach Vermot* includes a list of floods, earthquakes and fires (with illustrations by Robida) and predicts more of the same for the following year. There was also a brief fashion for 'cosmic clouds', which could cause a variety of disasters if Earth passed through them. J. H. Rosny Aîné's *La Force mystérieuse* (1913) depicts a situation in which the planet's trajectory disturbs another, totally different world and produces terrible and inexplicable upheavals before the earth leaves the dangerous zone. A similar novel, Arthur Conan Doyle's *The Poison Belt*, appeared in the same year. This time the danger came in the form of a toxic cloud (a fictional transcription of the very real fear aroused by cyanogen-laden tail of Halley's comet).

The American writer Garrett Serviss, in *The Second Deluge* (1911), gave the universal flood scenario a twist. Whiston, we may remember, used a comet as a causal factor; Serviss imagines a gigantic cloud charged with water vapour, which meets the orbit of our planet. As it condenses, torrential rain raises sea levels until the continental landmasses are completely submerged. A thousand men and women of different nationalities and occupations are selected to live in a new Ark, built by an American in order to repopulate the world after the water has subsided. This kernel of humanity meets a much larger group, three million Americans who have taken refuge in the Rocky Mountains. Civilization, therefore, gets off to a new start on the best possible basis!

We should not confuse our genres and mix scientific hypotheses with fiction. But we cannot completely separate them either. By 1900, every form of intellectual and artistic production indicated that western civilization was experiencing a crisis in its development, a malaise expressed through an imagined catastrophe. Was this anxiety justified? Yes and no. None of the imagined cosmic dangers materialized but the world went through a troubled period that was almost as dramatic as the prophesied cosmic upheaval.

However, we should take the broader view. The history of humanity is characterized by an endemic anxiety (aggravated by periods of tension or crisis) when confronted with a threat to the balance of nature. It is as if something or someone is remorselessly trying to sabotage the world's driving force – and particularly its climate.

SIX

The Global Warming Dossier

THE TECHNOLOGICAL FLOOD

Despite every pessimistic prediction, Western civilization did not collapse. It did pass through some dangerous times; two World Wars, economic crises, totalitarian regimes and other pressures seemed partly to confirm the pessimistic forecasts. But technological progress was not impeded; economic growth resumed on an even more spectacular scale after the Second World War while democracy (in its Western, social-liberal form) also made advances. The latter half of the century, from 1950 to 2000, saw the highest growth figures ever recorded, an extraordinary acceleration of history. The pace of structural transformation shaped the tone of the era even more than sudden growth. This pace shows no signs of slowing down – quite the opposite, in fact. A new world is being created before our eyes, almost from one day to the next. The civilization of tomorrow – and this tomorrow is close – will be marked by ever-increasing technological sophistication and a new constellation of values and modes of behaviour. It may detach us almost completely from history as we have known it.

Nineteenth-century humanity, divided between the dream of a radiant future and the nightmare of a technological apocalypse, had been dazzled by the relatively modest beginnings of the acceleration phase. We live with the same logic of the future but it has assumed a much more powerful form: the human species will either succeed in dominating the universe or it will destroy itself. A new situation has come about, and has invested pessimistic predictions with clearer definition and greater urgency. For the first time in history, catastrophe scenarios based on humanity's ability to trigger the forces of destruction have become plausible. This goes far beyond anything imagined at the turn of the century, when sensitivities were attuned to cosmic and natural disasters. An incipient anti-utopianism had drawn attention to the possible drift towards a world dehumanized by technology, but technology had not yet been seen as an agent that might destroy not only the human soul but the entire human race, or at least might completely disrupt conditions of life on the planet. This is the new danger, the technological 'flood' of the future.

The first instrument in this panoply of destruction was the atomic bomb, shortly to be followed by its perfected version, the nuclear weapon. The destruction of Hiroshima on 6 August 1945 heralded the advent of a new era. It divided the world into two hostile camps. The Cold War lasted from the end of the Second World War to the fall of communism in 1989 and it maintained, particularly in the 1950s and 1960s, a high level of psychosis shaped by the threat of a new war whose destructive potential would be infinitely superior to that of all previous conflicts. Today's historians have access to a thoroughly documented and comprehensive 'nuclear dossier', a mass of scientific studies, strategic simulations, novels and films. The worst-case scenario envisaged the total destruction of humanity. Most hypotheses, however, focused on incomplete 'ends of the world', similar to the biblical Flood. Technological civilization might be wiped out but the survivors would pick up the threads.[1]

Climatic upheavals and nuclear cataclysms go well together. Atomic strikes might shatter society and decimate the human race but the aftermath, atmospheric and climatic degradation, could be even worse. In the early 1980s, Richard Turco, Carl Sagan and other American scientists formulated the concept of a 'nuclear winter'.[2] Their model was simple and coherent: nuclear explosions would create a dust cloud which would gradually cover the planet and block out the sun's rays. The Earth would be plunged into a 'Siberian' winter, with midsummer temperatures of -30°c in the temperate regions of the northern hemisphere.

The concept of 'nuclear winter' is closely linked to a similar climatic upheaval known as the 'winter of the comet'. Sixty-five million years ago, a comet or an asteroid struck the Earth; its impact projected an immense quantity of dust into the atmosphere and caused a prolonged glacial winter. This led to the extinction of the dinosaurs. There was no technology at the time: comets did the damage. There is no need for a comet today: we can do the job just as well ourselves. The same physical and climatological mechanism that wiped out the dinosaurs can also wipe out the human race. However, not all scientists accept that a comet led to the extinction of the dinosaurs while humanity, on the other hand, still exists.

As it was quite natural for Russians and Americans to think in opposite terms, a Russian scientist came up with the precise opposite of nuclear winter. Nuclear detonations would cause temperatures to rise, which would in turn lead to the melting of the glaciers, rising sea levels and almost universal flooding. Burning, freezing or drowning – the human race did not have much to look forward to.

Less than twenty years after the début of the nuclear fear, technology spawned another and apparently equally serious danger: the deterioration of the natural environment. In some respects, it was more disturbing than the nuclear threat. Nuclear war might never happen but pollution is a permanent phenomenon, a seemingly inevitable product of technological civilization, or at least of the type of civilization we have engineered.

Rachel Carson sounded the alarm in *Silent Spring* (1962). This American biologist challenged the use of pesticides, particularly DDT, heavily used at the time but since banned in many countries. Carson believed that the war against insects, conducted in order to protect crops and stimulate agricultural production, would lead to the opposite result, for the insects were actually thriving in an already poisoned environment. The imminent risk of killing off nature would leave us to face a future bereft of flowers and birds, a succession of sad and silent springs. This was only the beginning of the great wave of ecological anxiety that swept across the world in the 1960s and 1970s. It seemed increasingly obvious that man's industrial, agricultural and transport activities were seriously degrading the soil, oceans and atmosphere, as well as indirectly affecting his own biology and the achievements of civilization.

The psychosis reached a peak around 1972. In addition to the threat of nuclear war and the continuing degradation of the environment, many other factors seemed to be contributing to a perverse system of self-destruction. Nothing was working properly anymore or, more precisely, everything was working too fast; we were hurtling towards the edge of an abyss. *The Limits to Growth*, the celebrated Club of Rome report compiled by a team from the Massachusetts Institute of Technology headed by Dennis Meadows, appeared in 1972. The book claimed that five closely related factors – food, population, industrial production, emissions and pollution – would combine to create a destructive dynamic. The human race was multiplying too rapidly, food and primary materials were becoming scarcer and the environment was in the process of 'cracking'. Civilization would soon collapse, probably well before 2100. Moreover, resources were running out. There was enough iron ore for 93 years but aluminium would run out in 31 years, natural gas in 22 and oil in 20 (which meant that the post-1992 world, in which we are living today, would be deprived of oil; so much the better, some would argue – there would be less conflict and less pollution!). The only sensible solution would be to stop the engine, an option expressed by the acronyms ZEG and ZDG: Zero Economic Growth and Zero Demographic Growth – in other words, a world fixed in its present state.

Barry Commoner, an American expert on natural and technological disasters, adopted a similar tone in *The Closing Circle: Nature, Man and Technology* (1972). According to Commoner, if the industrialized world continued on its present course it would reach the point of no return in 20 to 50 years' time. Technological civilization would then collapse and the survivors would return to a savage state. However, as industry had ceased to exist, pollution levels would fall and the cycle could begin again.

The Club of Rome report was bitterly contested as soon as it was published. The already classic dispute between critics and supporters of 'progress' or, to be more exact, of unlimited technological and economic growth, had acquired a new context. As more than 30 years have already passed, it is quite apparent that oil and other primary materials are lasting longer than the report's authors believed. In the short term, the threats they envisaged have not materialized. Obviously, they could be proved right (fully or partially) in the longer term, or completely wrong. The collapse of technological civilization proclaimed by Commoner does not seem about to happen either, although the respite he gave us is almost over.

ICE AGE OR 'HEAT DEATH'?

Climate inevitably features in the catalogue of misfortunes resulting from technological recklessness and abuse of the environment. About 1970 we were presented with two completely opposite but equally vivid scenarios.

We are already acquainted with the first and risk becoming even more familiar with it. This is global warming, the result of greenhouse-gas emissions, formed chiefly of carbon dioxide but also other gases such as methane and nitrous oxide. When these gases are concentrated in the atmosphere they trap most of the long-wave radiation emitted by the Earth, prevent it from escaping into space and the temperature therefore rises. Fossil fuels are the main culprits, principally coal, oil and natural gas. The combined use of these primary materials dramatically increased in the twentieth century, particularly during the latter half. Energy production, industry and transport are the three most polluting sectors, followed by domestic heating. Nor is agriculture innocent; it may produce less carbon dioxide but it 'enriches' the atmosphere with methane (a by-product of cattle-raising, more precisely, of the digestion of ruminants) and nitrous oxide from fertilizers. The greenhouse effect was known in theory by about 1895, when the Swedish scientist Svante Arrhenius (1859–1927) made the connection between CO_2 and atmospheric temperature. According to his calculations, reducing the level of CO_2 would cool the planet, while doubling it would raise the global temperature by 5-6°C.

The opposite scenario is, of course, global cooling. Besides greenhouse gases, technological civilization also contaminates the atmosphere with what are known as 'aerosols', very fine liquid or solid particles produced by industrial activity, agriculture, traffic, quarrying etc. These are complemented by sulphates and nitrates from sulphur dioxide and nitrogen oxide emissions. The particles filter solar radiation and reduce its energy. They also form kernels of condensation for water vapour and lead to cloud formation, which in turn screens out the sun; although the clouds can sometimes contribute to warming.

Given that a certain amount of atmospheric pollution is inevitable, scientists in the early 1970s began to consider the possibility of balancing the two tendencies in order to neutralize their effects. In fact, if we look at the global temperature curve for the twentieth century, we note that the initial increase recorded between 1910 and 1945 was followed by a relatively stable period until about 1975; indeed, temperatures fell slightly in comparison with the maximum recorded in the early 1940s. This pattern encourages a range of hypotheses: increased warming, increased cooling, or a balance of the two. Some scenarios, adapted to reflect the general neurosis of the age (the confrontation between the two superpowers, the nuclear threat, the ecological crisis), are remarkably dramatic.

Gordon Rattray Taylor's *The Doomsday Book: Can the World Survive?* generated some publicity when it appeared in 1970. It is typical of the more dramatic approach and the author's extensive list of potential catastrophes leaves little room for optimism. The book naturally discusses climate and the two contradictory tendencies. 'Heat death', warmly recommended by some of the experts cited by Taylor, is dealt with first. It is attributed to the greenhouse effect and the changes man has wrought on the planet's landscape, all of which have an adverse effect on its *albedo* (the ratio between the quantity of radiation falling on to a surface and the amount that is reflected). Short-term rises in temperature could vary between 10 and 20°c. In such conditions the poles would become as hot as the tropics are today, while the latter would prove inhospitable to life forms other than lizards and insects. Most fish species would die in the overheated oceans. This grim process will be accomplished in precisely 26 years' time. But it does not stop there: in 70 years' time, heat death will have put paid to every life-form on the planet – so farewell to the insects. However, a more optimistic version suggests that the end might take a little longer to arrive – as much as 150 years! The opposite scenario was no more appealing. In fact, it seemed to hasten the end. Temperatures would drop by 1.5°C in 1970; 4°C in 1975; 5°C in 1977 and so on. The new ice age would begin before 1980.[3]

Humanity was apparently already condemned to death; only one small detail remained to be settled – the means of execution. The folly of these extreme scenarios is clear to us today. Such fantasies should at least encourage scientists and popular science writers to exercise a little more caution.

SIX DEGREES WARMER: *towards a new climatic order*

The oscillation between scenarios that prevailed in 1970 has now vanished and the global warming argument has emerged victorious. It matches, one might say, the way climate is actually evolving. It has to be accepted that global temperatures began to rise again between 1970 and 1975. This seems to indicate that of the two series of polluting factors, that which determines temperature increase has gained the upper hand. Heat death has not yet arrived, nor is it forecast for tomorrow, or even for the next century. Nevertheless, the world is getting warmer (an estimated average increase of 0.6°C over the course of the twentieth century, of which 0.5°C applied to the period 1950–2000).

It should be pointed out that there is also a 'natural' interpretation of global warming, one which centres on a possible increase in solar radiation. The variations in the parameters of the earth's orbit (revealed in the 1930s by the Serbian astronomer Milutin Milankovitch), the sun's activity and a complex set of phenomena linked with geophysical factors like ocean currents and volcanic activity offer an explanation for the climatic fluctuations before our epoch. But as the global warming model developed, it had to take account of the massive contribution made by human activity.

Since 1990, each heightened forecast has exacerbated our anxiety. The current range of scenarios is based on a generally accepted estimate, which sees global temperatures rising between 1.5 and 6°C by 2100, although there is a tendency to privilege the higher figure. Furthermore, the averages reflect a highly unequal distribution of heat, suggesting that the poles will warm up much more than equatorial regions, land masses more than oceans, winters more than summers and nights more than days. An average rise of 3°C might be reflected in an increase of 6°C over the continents. We are already envisaging winter temperatures rising by 10° in the Arctic zone and 5°C in the temperate regions. If we remember that climate oscillations throughout the historical era were confined to about 1°C, we can judge the scale of the predicted upheavals. During the last ice age, average temperatures were 5°C below their current average and the consequences are well known; what would happen if they rose by 5o?

Like estimates of the extent of global warming, possible consequences vary from one interpretation to another.[4] It is widely believed that the march towards a 'new climatic order' will be accompanied by extreme disruption. There will be no measured or coordinated rise in temperature, but a breakdown of existing balances. There will be considerable atmospheric instability and stark contrasts from one region to another. Heat and evaporation will generate more rain but rainfall patterns will show greater contrasts than exist today. Equatorial regions and northern Europe will become much wetter while those around latitude 30°, which already suffer from a lack of rain, will become drier. Floods will become increasingly frequent, as will droughts. Atmospheric circulation will gain in 'tension', entailing more frequent and more powerful storms. Heat will force the ecosystems, vegetation and animals of the northern hemisphere to migrate further north. Such massive displacement cannot occur without structural damage. The danger is that the already precarious natural balance will be completely shattered. It is thought that certain trees and forest ecosystems are likely to disappear. Viruses and microbes could thrive in the new conditions and encourage the proliferation of various diseases. Malaria, almost eradicated by the draining of marshlands, is likely to return if the marshes re-form due to excessive rainfall. According to an article in the January 2004 issue of *Nature*, one million species of animal and plant life will be under threat of extinction by 2050!

We should not forget the predictable rise in sea levels, fed by melting ice from sources such as the Alpine glaciers, Greenland and Antarctica. Sea levels rose by 120 metres at the end of the last ice age. At its height, the contours of the continents were very different from today; England, for example, was still linked to France. If all the planet's ice melted, sea levels would rise by an estimated 70 metres. The Netherlands would cease to exist, as would many densely populated coastal regions. New York would be reduced to a few skyscrapers protruding above the waves. London would suffer a similar fate and Paris would be partially affected. (Parisians could take refuge on the Butte Montmartre or the Montagne Sainte-Geneviève as the water would not reach that far.) However, this is a science fiction scenario or at worst, a very distant possibility. Most current estimates indicate a rise of between 40 and 50 centimetres by 2100 (considerably less than the 3.5 metres predicted in 1980). This may seem insignificant but it is enough to cause problems for populations living at sea level (the atolls of the Pacific are in greatest danger). Moreover, it is only the beginning. Global warming and its consequences might not end in 2100 and could intensify in the following centuries. Scenarios for the year 3000 already exist, predicting rises in sea level of about 10 metres.

The fact is that, irrespective of scientific data, universal flooding has been one of the mainstays of the catastrophic imagination since the biblical Flood. As we are discussing fiction, we should cite J. G. Ballard's *The Drowned World* (1962), which appeared a few years before global warming was attributed to human activity. Ballard set his novel in the third millennium: the approach of Earth and sun has dramatically altered climatic conditions; part of the planet lies under water and the rest is covered in tropical forest. The image of submerged cities, the top of a building poking up here and there, may seem premonitory for those who privilege this version of the future.

Science fiction is sometimes overtaken by virtual reality. An exhibition on global warming was organized at the Cité des Sciences in Paris in the autumn of 2003. It featured some very convincing images of Paris in 2100 (already partially submerged!) and, for good measure, Sydney engulfed by a gigantic fire. It all seemed very real!

EL NIÑO

As if we did not have enough to worry about, another disturbing phenomenon had been making its presence felt for some time. Its name, El Niño, is already familiar.[5] El Niño's history long predates that of the human race but little attention was paid to it until the concept of a global climate came into existence. Indeed, there was a time – not so long ago – when Europe had its *own* climate, which had nothing to do with that of other regions. If distant and exotic regions were subject to climatic excesses, that was exactly why they were exotic and home to different peoples and civilizations. But the notion of globalization has been gaining ground for some time now, not just in an economic sense, but meteorologically, too. Sir Gilbert Walker, who headed the Indian Meteorological Service at beginning of the twentieth century and became professor of meteorology at the University of London, was one of the pioneers of 'global climate' theory. He observed that the monsoons of southern Asia were related to the global configuration of atmospheric circulation.

Thus, scientists were approaching El Niño. The breakthrough came in 1982, when extreme weather swept across the Western world, particularly the United States, and California was struck by devastating hurricanes. There was also flooding in China and drought in Australia. The origin of these disturbances was sought and found in the waters of the planet's biggest ocean. El Niño signifies a periodic reversal of ocean currents in the eastern Pacific. Instead of the usual cold water, a warm current reaches the Peruvian coast in winter, entailing a reversal of climatic tendencies in the region: normally arid regions experience abundant rain. As a local phenomenon, it was well known to the inhabitants of the region. The new interpretations, however, accorded it an incomparably greater role. Besides rain, it is now seen as being responsible for droughts in other parts of the continent as well as in the Sahel, India, Australia and Indonesia. The waters of the Pacific thus hold one of the principal keys to the Earth's climatic mechanism.

Phenomena long considered separate thus acquired an unexpected degree of coherence. In 1982, scientists went back ten years to 1972, a year noted for unusual and dramatic weather, particularly the catastrophic drought in the Sahel and similar episodes in South America, India, Australia and China. These events were linked and retrospectively attributed to El Niño. Once the cause had been identified, it became easier to predict its behaviour. These studies proved of practical value in 1997–8 when El Niño returned to California, bringing with it the usual rain and storms. There was less damage this time since the bad weather had been expected and precautions taken.

Given the tendency to interpret climate in global terms, scientists could not fail to make the connection between El Niño and global warming. They feared the potential impact of increasing climatic instability on El Niño's already capricious behaviour. The phenomenon could become even more difficult to predict and control.

The past is just as open to question as the present and the future. Every discovery has the potential to establish a new direction in the interpretation of history. This is what Brian Fagan, an anthropologist at the University of California at Santa Barbara, suggests in *Floods, Famines and Emperors: El Niño and the Fate of Civilizations* (1999). El Niño is presented as a key to the history of humanity. Its torrential rains and prolonged droughts have been wreaking havoc since the dawn of time. To some extent, primitive man made a better job of protecting himself from these onslaughts than we do today. When he found the climatic situation too harsh, he 'changed his address' by moving from one region to another. This type of solution is not available to developed civilizations. Some are able to resist the hazards of the weather more or less effectively. Others collapse, paralysed by the accretion of demographic, economic and social tensions. El Niño is not primarily responsible for the demise but it does deliver the *coup de grâce*. Egypt was severely damaged by drought during the Middle Kingdom period (*c*.2040–1640 BC), but its ruling class proved equal to confronting the crisis, a long-distance effect of El Niño. The Moche civilization in Peru and the Mayan Empire in Mexico both perished, the former through excessive rainfall and the latter through severe drought. Their inflexible social and governmental systems prevented them from successful adaptation. And what does the future hold for technological civilization? Fagan provides no answer. It depends on our ability to rise to the challenge. One thing is certain: El Niño will continue to strike.

REINVENTING CIVILIZATION

How are we to deal with this situation? If we take the most dramatic global warming scenarios seriously and accept their predictions, the only reasonable conclusion is to attack the causes. That means reducing the emission of greenhouse gases as much as possible. Several international conferences have been set up to devise an appropriate strategy, including the Rio summit in 1992 and the Kyoto meeting in 1997. Signatories to the Kyoto protocol pledged a 6–8 per cent reduction from their 1990 emission levels by 2012. Given the scale of the problem, such a step is hardly adequate. In the first place, the proposed cuts seem too feeble to be effective in stopping the accumulation of carbon dioxide in the atmosphere. They would barely slow down our march towards the abyss. Second, these modest 'commitments' are often broken. Moreover, many industrial countries, notably the United States, have not even ratified the protocol. The Americans argue against it on a number of grounds: the global warming thesis is scientifically unproven; adherence to the protocol would harm its economy; developing countries are exempt despite the fact that their drive to industrialization will increase carbon dioxide emissions. The fact remains that after a slight reduction of 3 per cent during the 1990s, emissions are increasing at a rate that could reach 17 per cent by 2010.

If we accept the arguments we should be adopting much stricter measures than those employed up to now. We should be reducing the use of fossil fuels to the lowest possible level and looking at abandoning them altogether. Naturally, proposals vary according to the gravity of the danger, which varies from one climatic model to another. For an example of the most drastic version, I will turn to Jean-Marc Jancovici, a French engineer specializing in energy problems and the greenhouse effect and author of *L'Avenir climatique* (2002). Jancovici supports the most extreme global warming scenario and the remedies he suggests are, of course, equally extreme.

His logic is impeccable – provided that the premise is correct! The aeroplane and the car are incontestably the two biggest emitters of CO_2. They are also perhaps the two most powerful symbols of our technological universe and the way we conduct our lives. Whether we like it or not, we will simply have to get rid of them. The private car will become a thing of the past as walking or cycling can easily replace it. If we want to go a little further we can use the underground system or the bus or – a small concession – share a small pool of cars. Trains and boats will take care of long-distance travel, heralding a return to the heyday of the *Titanic* and the Orient Express. Air travel will be reduced to no more than 10 per cent of its current level.

The question of habitat will be addressed at the same time. This will spell the end for the great urban centres and their vast transport networks, those voracious consumers of energy and bottomless sources of carbon dioxide. Towns will become smaller, more densely populated and more numerous. The production of materials like steel, glass, plastic, cement and paper will decrease as less energy is burned, while their prices will necessarily increase. We will just have to get used to consuming less. As a consequence there will be fewer private houses and we may have to live in closer proximity to each other. The fewer surfaces there are to heat, the less demand there is for heating. Food will not escape this radical reorganization; a diet containing less meat is recommended, because cattle produce methane gas. And so it goes on – nothing will be as it was before. The drawbacks are so obvious that they are not worth describing in detail. But what are the advantages? The most important is that we will put a stop to the greenhouse effect. And over time, we will probably enjoy the benefits of a healthier lifestyle: less agitation, noise and stress, more physical exercise and more time to ourselves, and so on.

But we are still left with the problem of energy consumption. Even if we drastically reduced our use of energy, we would not be able to get it below a certain level. Moreover, what form of energy should we use if fossil fuels are banned? Electricity itself is not necessarily cleaner; most of it is currently produced by burning coal and oil. Wind and solar power are sometimes suggested as alternative sources but would only offer a limited complement. The only credible alternative is nuclear energy. This is the cleanest form of energy, at least in terms of greenhouse gas emissions. But the fear of nuclear contamination (the 'Chernobyl syndrome') is as great as the fear aroused by global warming. Environmentalists do not like coal and oil but they do not like the atom either. For some experts, including Jancovici, this is still the lesser evil: CO_2 will inevitably lead us to disaster, but nuclear accidents are avoidable.

We can discuss this project from several angles. We can be for or against it. But there is not much opportunity to move the discussion beyond the academic level. This is for the good (or bad) reason that such a change of direction will never happen; it would be totally contrary to current developments. How can we reduce air traffic by 90 per cent when it continues to increase from year to year? It would be difficult even to confine it to its present level. How can we dismantle great urban conurbations when they are still expanding? We have become accustomed to a kind of freedom and well-being that presupposes ownership of a house and a car at the very least. Who is prepared to give up such comforts? And how? It is the kind of decision that would have to be authoritatively imposed on the human race as a whole. Even if it was our only chance of survival, I fear it would not work.

And supposing the alarm were false or at least exaggerated? What a nightmare it would be, in effect, to overturn conditions of life on the planet in order to escape a danger that may not exist, or may be less harmful than the means employed to combat it.

DOWNWARD REVISION: *global warming with a 'human face'*

Bjorn Lomborg takes a very different position in *The Sceptical Environmentalist: Measuring the Real State of the World*, one of the publishing sensations of 2001. Lomborg is not an opponent of the global warming theory nor of the environmental movement. A Danish professor of statistics, he began his career as a militant environmentalist. However, he has distanced himself from the kind of 'catastrophism' that has become synonymous with environmentalism in some quarters. According to Lomborg, the current state of the planet may leave a lot to be desired but it is far from disastrous. His chosen weapons are a broad range of comparative, long-term statistics which indicate that the planet has evolved rather favourably over the last hundred years. The figures contradict the claim that pollution is ruining the biological condition of the human species. Humanity has never been as healthy as it is today. Mortality rates have fallen and life expectancy has spectacularly increased. Cancers are more numerous simply because (smoking aside) there are more elderly people who are likely to develop the disease; in 1900, most people died before they got cancer. Large-scale deforestation seems to be another myth: statistics show that tree-cover remained remarkably stable from 1850 to 2000. Most European forests were cut down in the Middle Ages and at the beginning of the modern era. Tree-felling in America and the rest of the world peaked in the nineteenth century. Lomborg is moderately optimistic on all fronts and believes that progress will continue as before. Contrary to another false alarm, there will be no lack of energy resources. Man, in the final analysis, seems quite capable of managing growth and knows how to avoid its pitfalls.

As for global warming, Lomborg draws attention to the bad habit of 'rounding up' figures, a practice which adds an extra percentage to imagined dangers. While the range of possible scenarios is quite broad, the most popular are usually those that quote the highest figures. When variants are taken into account, the estimated thermal surplus for 2100 is put at 1.5°c to 6°c. However, the higher figure (if it is not even greater – some people speak of 9°c!) clearly has more appeal than less dramatic variants. Another illusion stems from the presumed truth of the scenarios. It is not a matter of 'truths' at all but, more modestly, of simulations, virtual models that may or may not be confirmed by future events. A computer does not say 'this is truth'. It is a counting machine, not a crystal ball in which the future may be read. It merely provides answers according to the parameters and algorithms programmed into it. The scientist controls the machine.

Lomborg does not dispute the existence of the greenhouse effect, nor the extent to which humans are responsible for it. However, he tends to favour a moderate warming scenario that foresees increases in temperature of between 2°c and 2.5°c over the next hundred years, figures that are consistent with the Massachusetts Institute of Technology model. Most importantly, he suggests that the consequences do not necessarily have to be catastrophic. According to his own simulations, global warming will have no significant effect on food production, atmospheric stability, the power and frequency of storms or the spread of contagious diseases. He accepts that warming will produce wetter conditions but maintains that a wealthier world will be better able to cope with rising sea levels and increased flooding. Clearly, adapting to the new conditions will come at a price. But it will be less than the price of combating, with limited success, the climatic developments currently under way. Industrialized countries might even benefit from a temperature rise of 2–3°c, which would bring milder winters and better conditions for agriculture (in effect, winters rather than summers would become warmer). On the other hand, developing countries would find it more difficult to adapt. The good news is that the planet will become greener through the influence of three combined factors: heat, carbon dioxide and rainfall. It should be noted that CO_2 acts like a fertilizer, which explains the stimulating effects it has on certain plants and agricultural crops (one science-fiction scenario depicts a return of the gigantic vegetation that flourished in the carboniferous era thanks to a surplus of CO_2). The Earth's biomass – assaulted and eroded by human activity – could increase by 40 per cent in the next century and reach almost prehistoric levels. Far from acting as an agent of destruction, technological civilization could restore nature to its original parameters, a prospect that environmentalists should be celebrating!

Lomborg concludes that although global warming constitutes a threat, we can confront it and turn it to our advantage. Moreover, it is not the most serious problem we currently face. Economic development in both poor and rich countries is vital. Application of the Kyoto protocol would swallow up a great deal of money and yield inconclusive results. The money would be better spent on development aid for the third world, which would then be able to combat global warming more successfully. We should also increase investment in research and in the exploitation of new forms of energy like solar radiation, nuclear fusion, etc. We should aim to free ourselves from our dependency on fossil fuels as soon as possible. The correct response to the climatic challenge is not less technology and development but more of both.[6]

Lomborg is not alone in seeking to play down the consequences of a possible global warming. The Massachusetts Institute of Technology (MIT) has opted for a moderated variant of global temperature increase that amounts to no more than 2.5°C over the next century. According to scientists at MIT, there is a hundred to one chance of a 5.8°C increase (the same odds as are offered for an almost negative increase of 0.3°C). The obviously rounded-up figure of 6°c is, however, the figure most often mentioned in discussions of global warming.

Some commentators appeal to history in order to demonstrate that moderate rises in temperature need not inevitably lead to calamity. They reiterate the argument that the 'little climatic optimum' stimulated European economic growth between the tenth and thirteenth centuries, while the Little Ice Age was associated with agricultural problems, food shortages and epidemics.

Whatever the case, economists are clearly less 'heated' in their debates than climatologists.[7] Several of the former have warned of upheavals that might owe less to the greenhouse effect than to the vast and hastily implemented measures designed to avert it. They believe the cost of global warming should be estimated on a country-by-country and sector-by-sector basis. Some countries and sectors might suffer while others would gain. Russia and Canada would benefit from a milder climate. According to some projections, even the United States could come out well. Europe might experience some difficulties but India and Africa would bear the brunt of change. However, provided that the worst effects are mastered, the global assessment could turn out to be positive, particularly for the agricultural sector.

Research released in 2003 tends to support the scenario outlined above. American scientists have calculated that part of the 'value' of the growth of agricultural production recorded in the American Midwest during the 1980s and 1990s can be attributed to the greenhouse effect. We should also note the annual 1 per cent increase in the biomass of the Amazonian forest. Scientists are already beginning to wonder if this development, which is partly due to CO_2, might not also be contributing to a reduction in CO_2 levels; plant life, as we know, absorbs the gas. Perhaps the notion of such perfect self-regulation is too good to be true.[8]

There is also good news from the glaciers and oceans. Glaciologists assure us that the dreaded universal flood is nothing more than the product of an overwrought imagination. I shall summarize their arguments.[9]

It is clear that mountain glaciers have already undergone considerable shrinkage. If they melted completely, the effect on sea levels would be practically nil. The Arctic ice field is composed of floating ice, which is obliged to conform to the Archimedean principle. Again, if it melted completely there would be no corresponding increase in sea levels. That leaves us with two continental ice caps: the Antarctic (90 per cent of the total) and Greenland (10 per cent). The disappearance of these ice caps would result in sea levels rising by 70 metres.

The Antarctic ice cap is divided into two very different complexes. The largest body of ice is found in the east and forms a massive carapace whose thickness ranges from one to five kilometres. It encompasses 85 per cent of the volume of the continent's ice and is by far the greatest single mass of ice on the planet. This mass has not changed significantly since the birth of Antarctica 60 million years ago. In other words, it has remained untouched by the climatic variations that have occurred since then. The temperature drops to -70°c in winter and hovers around -50°c in summer. It is unlikely to melt. That would require such a huge rise in global temperatures that we would all probably burn to death before the waters from the South Pole caught up with us. Paradoxically, global warming could even contribute to the growth of the ice cap as greater evaporation would lead to more snow.

A different situation prevails in western Antarctica. As its glacial layer is thinner and somewhat fragmented, it is more fragile and its edges are susceptible to crumbling. But for the moment the variations in the glacial mass are inconclusive and it would be unwise to relate them to global warming. Moreover, some estimates suggest that the ice cap might even have increased over the last twenty years. Greenland presents a similar profile; some parts of it may be affected by warming and others by cooling.

If the ice caps were to melt – although we have seen that this is hardly likely – the effect of this happening in western Antarctica would be to increase sea levels by five to seven metres, and in Greenland by four or five metres. A total of ten or twelve metres would obviously spell disaster for coastal regions. Miami and Bangkok would become 'undersea' cities. But current observations indicate that western Antarctica's annual contribution to sea level rise is 0.16mm and Greenland's 0.13mm. This is less than the mountain glaciers of Alaska, which might contribute as much as 0.27mm annually. These figures add up to barely half a millimetre. According to current trends, it amounts to five centimetres in 100 years. Even if the figure were several times higher, the possibility of a universal flood remains remote.

NO WARMER, NO COLDER

Critics of the concept of global warming, or of rising temperatures due to human activity, are fewer and do not receive much exposure in the media but still command attention. We should listen to what they have to say.[10] They contend that global warming is too recent for any valid conclusions to be drawn from it. Moreover, the estimated increase is quite modest: the average of 0.6°c recorded over the last hundred years is not exceptional when compared to other prehistoric or historical variations and offers no cause for alarm.

On the other hand, there is no perfect correlation between the warming curve and that of greenhouse gas emissions, particularly CO_2. A glance at these curves reveals that the global temperature began to rise from about 1850. It fluctuates slightly until 1910 and even dips towards the end of this period. The curve then rises sharply from 1910 to 1940–45, illustrating a rate of warming almost as fast as it is today. A new cooling phase set in during the early 1940s and lasted until just after 1970. After that the curve begins to climb and continues to do so.

Let us compare this curve with the one for CO_2 emissions. These were insignificant until 1900, which makes it difficult to suggest that they are the origin of global warming. There is a certain concordance from 1910 to 1940–45 but even so, the temperatures curve rises a lot faster than CO_2 emissions, which were still relatively modest. The emissions increase dramatically towards 1940–45 and reach a peak in 1970, the very period in which the temperature drops rather than continues to rise. In order to interpret this divergence, we can turn to another factor, the 'dust particles' which may be cooling the atmosphere. In fact, we are dealing with the most dynamic period in the history of western industrial development; besides CO_2 emissions, industry also polluted the atmosphere with its 'aerosols' and, even more, with nuclear explosions, which may aggravate the cooling process. Both CO_2 emissions and temperatures increase after 1975. But the period in question is really too short to allow firm conclusions to be drawn. The evidence does not provide us with a coherent and irrefutable model.[11]

The accuracy of meteorological recordings is also open to question. Only a complete and uniform 'inspection' of the planet could produce totally reliable results. This has never been possible. The continents have been monitored much more closely than the oceans, while developed countries have many more meteorological stations than poor countries. Furthermore, today's stations are different from those of a hundred years ago; some have closed down and others have been opened. As for the precision of recordings, those taken around 1900 served as benchmarks, but they are much less reliable than measurements taken today. An increasing number of stations are now located in or near great urban centres. Towns produce heat; temperatures in urban environments are generally higher than those in rural areas. Urban microclimates are increasingly common and can lead to further imprecision. There is too much imprecision, claim the critics of global warming, particularly as we are focusing on temperature variations measured in fractions of a degree.

Even if we accept a certain tendency towards warming, its relation to the causal effect of CO_2 is far from proven. The current rise in temperatures, like those noted at other times in history, might depend on natural and cosmic variations such as solar radiation, etc. The relative correspondence between the rise in temperature and the concentration of CO_2 in the atmosphere does not necessarily indicate a relationship of cause and effect. Some scientists are inclined to absolve CO_2 and point the finger at methane, which receives less publicity but which may be a major contributor to atmospheric pollution. So perhaps we have got the wrong enemy. We should not forget the opposite scenario either: that global warming itself is responsible for the increase of CO_2 in the atmosphere (because warmer water absorbs smaller quantities of carbon dioxide gas).

Perhaps we are a little too ready to treat warming as a global phenomenon. In fact, climate develops differently and in a bewilderingly contradictory way from one region to another. This emphasizes the importance of regional studies, but it is no easy task to collate such studies. In Iceland, for example, the west coast is cooling down while the east coast is getting warmer. Ukraine has become a little warmer and Scandinavia a little colder. The poles are behaving in a particularly paradoxical way. There is general agreement that warming should be more intense in the polar regions than elsewhere. The North Pole is obediently complying with this directive; Arctic summers are beginning to resemble summers as we know them; 40 per cent of the polar ice has disappeared over the last 50 years. What remains will disappear almost completely in 10 years or so, allowing the establishment of regular commercial seaways. Who would have believed that 20 years ago, when the Russians were dreaming of gigantic engineering projects to heat the Arctic waters? The ocean is now doing the job itself (assisted, perhaps, by our CO_2 emissions). The days of the ice-breaker seem to be over. There is now no call for intrepid navigators to risk their lives in an attempt to force a way through the famous north-east passage of Siberia or the north-west passage of Canada. This would be splendid but for the existence of the other pole. For the situation in Antarctica is very different: ice continues to accumulate and the temperature appears to be falling. What 'global' conclusion can we draw from such evidence?[12]

There remains the problem of the meteorological excesses of recent years. We have acquired the habit of blaming the greenhouse effect for heatwaves, storms and droughts. However, meteorologists point out that many recent events are no more extreme than their twentieth-century predecessors. We quickly forget the storms of the past and tend to regard the most recent as the most violent. On the other hand, a ten-degree temperature 'surge' (like the heatwave that overwhelmed western Europe in the summer of 2003) cannot be explained by a global increase, which is estimated to be less than one degree. And we should remember that we are not lacking in cold spells (although the summer of 2003 certainly enhanced our psychological perception that the world was heating up).

Sceptics argue not only that humanity's contribution to global warming has been exaggerated but that the phenomenon itself may be just a scenario. Given this possibility, we should be looking at alternative models which take into account heightened meteorological instability and more contrasted regional and seasonal behaviour such as wetter winters and drier summers. Such variations should be studied within the context of normal climatic parameters for, as knowledge currently stands, it would be unwise to go further.

If we take one step further we stumble upon the opposite scenario: we have good reason to be worried, but the danger comes from a new and possibly imminent ice age. If we look at the Quaternary's succession of glacial and interglacial phases (the former significantly longer than the warming phases), the indications are that the end of an interglacial era is approaching. Some climatologists, alert to the slightest sign, are concerned about the current expansion and stabilization of the Antarctic glaciers. A theory is also emerging that climate change occurs suddenly rather than gradually. If the process has already been triggered we might be leaving our comfortable interglacial period behind and slipping, day-by-day or year-by-year, into a new ice age. 'New York under the ice' is the 'glacial' version of the 'New York under water' headline promoted by advocates of the global warming thesis. A television documentary has explained in vivid detail how the skyscrapers would be reduced to rubble and displaced by masses of ice, like the boulders strewn across the region during the last ice age. If this is about to happen, we should be grateful for CO_2, methane and the greenhouse effect. The temperature rises caused by human activity will at least help us to slow down the predicted cosmic cooling and mitigate its effects.

European temperatures could still fall by several degrees, even without the advent of a new ice age. And strange as it may seem, this too would be due to global warming! If the Greenland ice cap melted it would swell the Atlantic with an immense quantity of fresh water. This would modify deep ocean circulation and could destabilize or even cancel out the warm Gulf Stream current. It is because of the Gulf Stream that temperatures on Europe's west coast are several degrees higher than those on America's northeast coast, although both are on the same latitude. So here is yet another paradoxical development: the warmer the climate becomes, the colder it will be in Europe.[13]

FROM CLIMATE TO IDEOLOGY

It is time to call a halt to this parade of scenarios. Five principal tendencies have emerged from our discussion and may be summarized thus: 1. Man is responsible for global warming; if we do not change our ways we may face catastrophe. 2. Man is responsible for global warming but if we manage it skilfully its effects need not be disastrous. Certain regions might even benefit from it. 3. Man is not responsible for global warming. 4. There is no such thing as global warming. 5. Certain signs point to an imminent global cooling phase, a prelude to a new ice age.

The first thesis – rising temperatures and the destructive effects of human activity – has achieved the greatest impact and has been responsible for the development of a kind of psychosis. It is worth asking why this should be so. The first possible answer is: because it is true. And as it is true, we should not be wasting our time and energy on further speculation; the future of the planet and the survival of civilization are at stake.

Only the future will tell us if this is the correct answer. In any case, it is not sufficient. In every era, including our own, truths are ignored or disputed while errors or illusions hold sway. Our search for an explanation must go beyond the factual basis of the theory and focus on the reasons for its dominance. Our interpretation must take into account both the way the imagination tends to work and the existing social, ideological and psychological context.

We have only to recall the attitudes I have traced step-by-step in this book. In the first place, we have the psychological element, the human propensity for catastrophism. A major upheaval captures our attention much more easily than the events of everyday life; it can even exercise a sort of fascination. In the second place, we have the cyclical model of history, that most ancient and durable of scenarios to which we always return, adapting it as we do. This can be summarized in the words: rise and fall (but the second term of this double metaphor is always stronger than the first; it is a constant presence, reminding us of the fragility of existence and the likelihood of a final reckoning). Apparently, we are already at the summit and it is not hard to guess the fate that awaits us. As we have already noted, the acceleration of history only exacerbates this tendency; it ceaselessly adds to our stock of anxieties. As history rushes on at an ever-greater pace, so do our fears.

There is no doubt that the current context is highly conducive to the spread of the most alarmist scenarios. Our attachment to models is one of the most influential factors and is worth closer examination. We are increasingly becoming tempted to confuse 'existing reality' with 'virtual reality'. Certainly, the 'model' is an indispensable scientific and investigative tool; reality is too vast, too complex and chaotic to approach directly. We have to revert to methodological intermediaries. Models are simplified, coherent and synthetic versions of a certain dimension of reality or deter-mined process. They are extremely useful as long as we remember that they are not the real thing: they are methodological fictions. If scientists sometimes fall into the trap of confusing them with real-ity, what should we expect from the general public? Particularly as all these exercises seem to become more elaborate and mathe-matically precise with each passing day. The computer reinforces this impression, and how could it be mistaken? Obviously, it does not make mistakes but it plays the scientist's game, it makes his findings seem even more rigorous.

However, reality is so complex and combines so many predictable and unpredictable factors that every forecast runs the risk of failing to observe actual developments. Most of the time we cannot even predict what will happen tomorrow. The history depicted in scenarios of the future has until now been an almost entirely inaccurate version of history. What happened to the 'radiant future' that Marx 'anticipated' so scientifically? H. G. Wells, a master of the genre, claimed in *Anticipations* (1903) that aviation would not play a significant role in the coming century. He also predicted the establishment of a universal language – French! Are we, with our computers, any closer to the truths of the future? We should at least entertain a few doubts. It seems that the more coherent a model or scenario is, the greater the risk that it will depart from reality, quite simply because reality is anything but simple or coherent.

Let us return to climate, for there are further questions to be asked. How can we place absolute confidence in the plethora of projections that rely on questionable data, extracted from a rigorously simplified context, while failing to take into account (as if they could!) the series of unknown factors that influence nature, technology and human behaviour? Whatever state the world is in by 2100, it will certainly not resemble the world predicted in any of the current scenarios. Nevertheless, the prestige of scientific models continues to grow.

Distortion and exaggeration come from many sources. We live in the age of the media and our imagination feeds on the information they supply. As a result, our tendency to focus on the unusual is heightened; it breaks the monotony of our existence. A moderate global warming scenario which predicts possibly benign or equivocal consequences is of no interest to the media. The most dramatic version will receive the most publicity. Sometimes the emphasis will shift from accelerating temperatures and their disastrous consequences to equally striking scenarios of the 'global warming is a lie' or 'new ice age imminent' variety. More neutral or balanced views such as 'we don't know' or 'there are other priorities in this world' seldom make news. The media are intent on dramatizing life and pursue that goal assiduously.

Turning to ideologies, we note that environmentalism occupies a privileged position. It is much more persuasive than the classic ideologies of the past such as liberalism, socialism and communism, all of which have been seriously eroded. There is less ideological tension in western democracies, which are accustomed to an attenuated mixture of liberalism and social democracy. But as one must always believe in something, environmentalism has come to fill a considerable part of the ideological vacuum. Its appeal is clearly justified by the actual or presumed upheavals occurring in the natural world, many of which can be attributed to the development of technological civilization. Environmentalism is not limited to ecological movements and parties. It takes the form of a sensibility that has infused the entire social body and political class. It is now 'politically correct' to think in environmental terms and 'politically incorrect' not to take into account the importance of ecology, or to deny it. In short, most of us are now environmentalists or claim to be so. When it is proclaimed that the planet is endangered, it would be difficult for a politician to deny or minimize that danger (at least in words, the usual substitute for effective measures).

Returning to the scientists, we find that not all of them are ardent supporters of the 'hard' version of global warming. However, the context favours this view. Some scientists might even go along with it with it for strategic reasons: cultivating a sense of danger or urgency can be a useful ploy; it focuses attention on your research and may help you to obtain funding. A 'soft' discourse does not get you very far. Scientists have their own lobby when it comes to climate.

In the final analysis, it is becoming difficult to appreciate what stems from disinterested expert opinion and what is attached to climate scenarios for one reason or another. In fact there are often several reasons for embellishment, including scientific strategy, environmental conviction, political demagoguery and media dramatization. Some analyses and projects get 'harder' as they progress from fundamental research to the less scrupulous domains of communication and decision-making. The possible becomes probable and probability becomes certainty.

It should be clear that both advocates and critics of the global warming thesis are responsible for framing the debate in ideological terms. Those who dispute the dangers of global warming generally favour the capitalist version of progress. Their views are liberal or even ultra-liberal and their faith in technology, industry, economic development and the profit motive is total. Society and environment are secondary concerns: all difficulties (including those associated with climate) will eventually be resolved by unrestrained and unlimited development. More concretely, many opponents of the idea of global warming have interests in the industries accused of generating of CO_2. This explains the attitude of the United States government; measures to combat global warming would jeopardize jobs and profits and put America's economy at risk.

The members of the other camp put society and environment before economic development. They oppose neo-liberal *laissez-faire* attitudes. They do not like globalization, which they see as leading to social and economic disparities and environmental disasters, including global warming. They do not like capitalism at all, particularly American capitalism. Anti-capitalist attitudes have survived the collapse of communism and the decline of revolutionary movements. This form of ideological restructuring – combating capitalism by global warming – would not have occurred to Lenin, Trotsky or Mao. The new activists are sometimes accused of demonizing CO_2 while deliberately ignoring methane, for reasons that have more to do with ideology than with the atmosphere. CO_2 symbolizes capitalist industry. Methane, chiefly produced by cattle and the cultivation of rice, symbolizes agricultural activity. The peasant and the Third World are potential allies so activists are hesitant about criticizing their 'emissions'.

I have drawn up my own two 'models'. Clearly, reality is more complex. Scientific arguments, ideological options, economic interests, political choices and media strategies can be combined in a multitude of permutations. Margaret Thatcher was one of the first political leaders to draw attention the greenhouse effect. However, her reasons for doing so were far from anti-capitalist. Her intervention came at a time when she was preparing to reduce coal production and close the pits. This is the explanation for her appeal on behalf of a healthier planet!

It is not for the historian to take sides in this debate. He lacks the competence to discuss the atmosphere. His only competence is to talk about the people who talk about the atmosphere. Global warming and global cooling are physical phenomena. But the battle over these real or presumed developments is a cultural and social phenomenon. In this sense at least, history and meteorology go hand-in-hand.

By Way of a Conclusion

The cultural history of climate I have just broadly outlined throws some light on the complex and sometimes curious relationship that exists between the real world and our imaginative capacity. Nothing is less debatable than the point of departure: climate is a massive presence and its parameters constitute one of the essential conditions for the evolution of life and of humanity. However, this axiom provides the basis for an incredible variety of interpretations and scenarios. The imagination thrives on reality but remodels it and invests it with multiple meanings.

It would be quite reasonable to expect that the advances made in every field of scientific endeavour should result in firmer conclusions about the nature of the world we live in. We know incomparably more than our ancestors did and our knowledge of our planet is now surely closer to the actual structure of things. But this is where the paradox arises: instead of bringing us closer to a definitive representation, greater knowledge simply engenders more interpretations and scenarios; those which concern the past as well as those which are designed to illuminate the future.

'Traditional' climatology was limited to the inventory of a few climatic zones that displayed fixed characters and corresponded, in human terms, with equally determined types of society and civilization. The range of combinations was quite narrow and stereotyped. Nowadays, however, climate is regarded as a dynamic model dependent on a multitude of factors. The social sciences, and history in particular, have in turn acquired a similar complexity. Once simple relationships have become extremely sophisticated. The proliferation of historical and climatic 'agents' has increased the range of potential connections.

We cannot expect more from history than it is capable of delivering. In the first place – and despite accumulating data and increasingly refined methods of investigation – no historical reconstruction will ever fully correspond with history as it actually happened; we must be content with a series of more or less complete images which have undergone varying degrees of simplification and distortion. Second, as historians are concerned with what no longer exists, they cannot experiment. The historical 'causes' that stimulate so much discussion have been identified through purely intellectual speculation; all interpretations are thus hypothetical and, while they may seem reasonable, their accuracy is impossible to verify. There is a huge variety of generalized explanations of history as a whole and of each of its segments, a diversity explicable in terms of the knowledge available, the scientific and cultural context, the impact of ideology and, of course, the historian's ingenuity. As our study of the past advances, more and more bridges are built between history and the other sciences, so that interpretative systems themselves become more diverse.

For a brief illustration of these considerations we can return to the studies of climatic oscillations. There can be no doubt that the identification of climate's historical evolutions has enriched our knowledge of the past. But, as is always the case with history, we are still far from a complete and accurate reconstruction. A controversy still rages over the scale of climatic variations, while their importance to a general system of historical interpretation is the source of even greater dispute. For example, how should we interpret the 'little climatic optimum' that occurred at the beginning of the second millennium? Did it correspond with a notable rise in temperature? If so, how great was the increase? Was the optimum confined to certain regions? Was it so insignificant that we should hesitate before classifying it as a distinct historical period? Did it play a leading role in the development of the West or was it of secondary importance, so imprecisely defined that it is hardly worth the historian's attention? There are a great number of possible and legitimate responses to all these questions.

If the past is so complicated, what can we say about the future, a totally unknown territory whose shape and details change from one prediction to the next? The future, like the past, has become more complex as the number of factors to be taken into account has increased (climate change now plays just as great a role as conflict between civilizations!). The number and variety of virtual representations increases exponentially. Every conceivable scenario comes into play, from the most optimistic – the continued flourishing of the human race – to the most pessimistic – a return to a state of savagery. Climate often seems to act as both a catalyst and a symbolic reference point in this game of simulations. In other words, tomorrow's world will be shaped by its climate. We will either moderate its excesses, perhaps even improve it through responsible action, or reduce it to chaos as we are sucked into its destructive maelstrom. Perhaps we are in the process of inventing a religion of climate. Who knows?

References

ONE Climate and People

1 Ovid, *Tristia, Ex Ponto*, trans. Arthur Leslie Wheeler (London, 1953),
   book 3, 10.

2 Diodorus of Sicily, *Bibliotheca Historica*, trans. C. H. Oldfather (London,
   1935), book 3, 34.

3 Ibid.

4 On the subject of 'zones' and other ancient representations of the Earth,
   see W.G.L. Randles, *De la Terre plate au globe terreste. Une mutation episto-
   mologique rapide 1480–1520* (Paris, 1980).

5 For 'zone' and 'climate' terminology see Germaine Aujac, 'Le vocabulaire
   géographique en Grèce ancienne', in *Documents pour l'histoire du vocabulaire scientifique* (Paris, 1982), no. 3, pp. 23–8.

6 The place of India in the imagination of the Classical world is illustrated
   by J. André and J. Filliozat, *L'Inde vue de Rome. Textes latins de l'Antiquité
   relatifs à l'Inde* (Paris, 1986).

7 For these prolongations of the zones theory, see Randles, *De la Terre*,
   pp. 33–41.

8 On the geographical distribution of otherness in the Greek imagination,
   see François Hartog, *Le Miroir d'Hérodote. Essai sur la representation de
   l'autre* (Paris, 1980). For a discussion of the invention and spatial
   distribution of the 'other', I suggest my own contribution: Lucian Boia,
   *Entre l'Ange et la Bête. Le Mythe de l'homme different de l'Antiquité à nos
   Jours* (Paris, 1995).

9 Herodotus, *The Histories*, trans. Robin Waterfield (Oxford, 1998), Book 2,
   35.

10 Hippocrates, *Airs, Waters, Places*, trans. W.H.S. Jones (London, 1923), paragraph 12.

11 Ibid., 23.

12 Ibid., 24.

13 Ibid., 19.

14 Solinus, *Polyhistor (De Mirabilibus mundi)* (Paris, 1847), chapter 16.

15 Strabo, *Geographica*, trans. Horace Leonard Jones (London, 1949), book 4, 5.4.

16 Details on the Ichthyophagi in Diodorus of Sicily, op. cit., 3, 15–20. For the Troglodytes, see Solinus, op. cit., chapter 32.

17 Hippocrates, *Airs, Waters, Places*, 16.

18 Aristotle, *The Politics*, 7, 7.

19 Strabo, *Geographica*, op. cit., book 2, 5, 26.

20 Ibid., book 2, 3, 7.

21 For the geographical and biological imagination of the Arabs, the chief reference is André Miquel, *La Géographie humaine du monde musulman jusqu'au milieu du XI siècle* (Paris and The Hague, 1975), vol. 2 ('Géographie arabe et representation du monde'), particularly the chapter entitled 'La Terre partagée', pp. 32–70.

22 Ibid., p. 321.

23 *Géographie d'Edrisi*, ed. P. Amédée Jaubert (Paris, 1836–40).

24 Ibn Khaldun, *The Muqaddimah, An Introduction to History*, trans. Franz Rosenthal (New York and London, 1958). The discussion and the passages cited are from vol. 1, pp. 167–73.

25 Jean Bodin, *Les Six livres de la République* (Paris, 1580), book 5, chapter 1, pp. 663–701.

26 Robert Burton, *The Anatomy of Melancholy* (Oxford, 1621).

27 A good and still useful synthesis of the different interpretations of the relationship between societies and the natural world may be found in Franklin Thomas, *The Environmental Basis of Society. A Study in the History of Sociological Theory* (New York and London, 1925).

TWO The Climate of the Philosophers: The Eighteenth Century

1 Jean-Baptiste Dubos, *Réflexions critiques sur la poésie et la peinture* (7th edition, Paris, 1702), vol. 2, section 15, 'Le Pouvoir de l'air sur le corps

humain prouvé par le caractère des Nations', pp. 266–7.

2 Ibid., vol. 2, section 17, p. 304.

3 Ibid., vol. 2, section 15, p. 275.

4 Ibid., vol. 2, section 19.

5 John Arbuthnot, *An Essay Concerning the Effects of the Air on Human Bodies* (London, 1733), chapter 4, paragraph 19.

6 Ibid., chapter 6, paragraph 20.

7 Montesquieu, *De l'esprit des lois – The Spirit of the Laws*, trans. Thomas Nugent (New York, 1949), book 14, chapter 2: 'Of the Difference of Men in Different Climates'.

8 Ibid., book 15, particularly chapter 5.

9 Ibid., book 16, chapter 2.

10 Ibid., book 16, chapter 8.

11 Ibid., book 17, chapters 3 and 4.

12 Ibid., book 19, chapter 14.

13 Ibid.

14 David Hume, *Political Essays*, ed. Knud Haakonssen (Cambridge, 1994); essay 12: 'Of National Characters', pp. 78–92.

15 William Wilkinson, *An Account of the Principalities of Wallachia and Moldavia* (London, 1820), pp. 128–9.

16 *L'Encyclopédie* (Paris, 1753), 'Climat', vol. 3, pp. 532–6.

17 Edward Gibbon, *Decline and Fall of the Roman Empire*, chapter 9.

18 Voltaire, 'Climat', in *Dictionnaire philosophique* (Paris, 1825), vol. 3, pp. 292–300.

19 Helvétius, *De l'esprit* (Paris, 1759), pp. 329–50.

20 Turgot, *Oeuvres* (Paris, 1808), vol. 2, pp. 179–80.

21 On the subject of imaginary representations of race during the Enlightenment, I refer the reader to my *Entre l'Ange et la Bête. Le Mythe de l'homme different de l'Antiquité à nos Jours* (Paris, 1995), pp. 109–72.

22 Linné, *Systema Natura*, 1735, thirteen editions to 1793.

23 Johann Friedrich Blumenbach, *De Generis Humani Varietate Nativa* (Göttingen, 1775).

24 Buffon, *Histoire naturelle* (1749–89). See the section *De l'homme*.

25 See Franklin Thomas, *The Environmental Basis of Society* (New York and London, 1925), pp. 270–71.

26 J.G. Herder, *Ideen zur Philosophie der Geschichte der Menscheit* (Riga, 1784–91), book 1, chapter 5.

27 Ibid., book 6, chapter 3.
28 Ibid., book 7, chapter 3.
29 See William Robertson, *History of America* (1777), book 4.
30 Gibbon, *Decline and Fall*, chapter 9.
31 Buffon, *Les Epoques de la Nature* (Paris, 1778), pp. 236–44; critical edition by Jacques Roger (Paris, 1962), pp. 211–15.

THREE   The North at the Zenith

1 Alexis de Tocqueville, *L'Ancien Régime et la Révolution* (1856), book 3, chapter 3.
2 For further discussion of the nineteenth-century racial ladder I refer the reader to my *Entre l'Ange et la Bête. Le Mythe de l'Homme different de l'Antiquité à nos jours* (Paris, 1995), pp. 176–85.
3 Modern studies of the 'psychology of peoples' owe much to Moritz Lazarus and Heymann Steinthal, *Zeitschrift für Völkerpsychologie und Sprachwissenschaft*, published from 1859. Among the most characteristic works, we should cite: Alfred Fouillée, *Tempérament et caractère selon les individus, les sexes et les races* (Paris, 1895); *Psychologie du people français* (Paris, 1898); *Esquisse psychologique des peoples européens* (Paris, 1903); Emil Boutmy, *Essai d'une psychologie politique du people anglais au XIV siècle* (Paris, 1901); *Eléments d'une psychologie politique du people américain* (Paris, 1902); Wilhelm Wundt: *Wölkerpsychologie* (Leipzig, 1904–10); *Elemente der Völkerpsychologie* (Leipzig, 1912).
4 Joseph Deniker, *Les Races et peoples de la Terre* (Paris, 1900), pp. 384–5.
5 George Bernard Shaw, 'Our Temperaments Contrasted' in the 'Preface for Politicians', *John Bull's Other Island* (various editions).
6 Buffon, *Histoire naturelle* (1749–89), section *De l'homme*.
7 Jules Verne, *Cinq semaines en ballon* (1863), chapter 3.
8 Charles Comte, *Traité de legislation* (Paris, 1826), vol. 2, p. 118.
9 Alexis de Tocqueville, *De la Démocratie en Amérique* (1835), vol. 1, part 2, chapter 9.
10 Henry Thomas Buckle, *History of Civilisation in England* (1857), vol. 1, chapter 2.
11 Hippolyte Taine, *Philosophie de l'art* (Paris, 1879, 3rd edition), p. 55.
12 Hippolyte Taine, *Philosophie de l'art en Grèce* (Paris, 1869), pp. 33–5.

13 Elisée Reclus, *Nouvelle géographie universelle* (Paris, 1875), vol. 1. p. 13.

14 Astolphe, Marquis de Custine, *La Russie en 1839* (Paris, 1843), letter 11.

15 For Ratzel's views on the relationship between man and environment see also his contribution to *Weltgeschichte* ed. H. F. Helmolt (English trans. *The History of the World*, London, 1901), vol. 1, chapter 3.

16 Ellen Churchill Semple, *Influences of Geographic Environment* (London and New York, 1914), p. 601.

17 Ibid., p. 620.

18 Ibid., p. 622.

19 Alexandre Xenopol, *La Théorie de l'histoire* (Paris, 1908), pp. 192–3.

20 Gobineau, *Essai sur l'inégalité des races humaines* (Paris, 1853), vol. 1, book 2, chapter 1.

21 Jean-Paul Demoule provides a good presentation of the Indo-European affair in his article 'Les Indo-Européens ont-ils existé?', *L'Histoire*, no. 28 (November 1980), pp. 108–20.

22 On Madison Grant and other American authors who supported the Nordic origins of the Aryans, see Franklin Thomas, *The Environmental Basis of Society* (New York and London, 1925), pp. 272–5.

23 Louis Agassiz, *Etude sur les glaciers* (Neuchâtel, 1840), particularly chapter 16: 'Des oscillations des glaciers dans les temps historiques'.

24 Alfred Angot, 'Etudes sur les vendages en France', *Annales du Bureau central météorologique de France* (1883).

25 Agassiz, *Etude sur les glaciers*.

26 Alfred Angot, *Traité élémentaire de Météorologie* (Paris, 1899), pp. 409–10.

27 Charles Fourier, *Théorie des quatre mouvements et des destinées générales* [1808] (Paris, 1966, pp. 41–52).

28 Frédéric Zurcher, *Les phénomènes de l'atmosphère* (Paris, 1862), principally pp. 15, 147 and 177–8.

29 *La Grande Encyclopédie* (Paris), vol. 11, 'Climat', p. 678.

30 Verne, *Cinq semaines en ballon*, chapter 16.

31 Camille Flammarion, *La Fin du monde* (Paris, 1894), pp. 247–51.

32 Albert Robida, '*Le Vingtième siècle*' et '*La Vie électrique*' (Paris, 1892), pp. 2–3.

33 Louis Figuier gives details of the plan for a Saharan sea in *Les nouvelles conquêtes de la science* (Paris, 1883–5), vol. 2. See the chapter 'La Mer intérieure africaine', pp. 747–808.

34 Angot, *Traité élémentaire de Météorologie*, pp. 410–11.

FOUR   The Changing Climate: The Twentieth Century

1 A detailed presentation of the work and conclusions of the American anthropological school may be found in Franklin Thomas, *The Environmental Basis of Society* (New York and London, 1925), pp. 277–93.

2 Paul Vidal de la Blache, *Principes de géographie humaine* (Paris, 1922), p. 24.

3 Alexander von Humboldt, *L'Asie centrale* (Paris, 1843), vol. 2, p. 295.

4 Ellsworth Huntington, *The Pulse of Asia. A Journey in Central Asia Illustrating the Geographic Basis of History* (Boston and New York, 1907), chapter 17: 'The Caspian Sea and its Neighbours', pp. 329–58.

5 Ibid., chapter 18: 'The Geographic Basis of History', pp. 359–85.

6 Ibid., p. 382.

7 Ibid., pp. 376–7.

8 Arnold J. Toynbee, *A Study of History* (abridgement of vols 1–6 by D. C. Somervell, New York and London, 1956), pp. 68–74.

9 Ibid., p. 95.

10 Ibid., pp. 96–9.

11 Ibid., p. 146.

12 For methods of climate history, see H. H. Lamb's detailed account, *Climate History and the Modern World* (New York and London, 1982; 2nd edition, 1995).

13 The great stages of climate development are discussed by Emmanuel Le Roy Ladurie, *Times of Feast, Times of Famine: A History of Climate Since the Year 1000* (New York, 1971); Lamb, *Climat, History and the Modern World*; Pierre Alexandre, *Le Climat en Europe au Moyen Age* (Paris, 1987); Pascal Ascot, *Histoire du climat* (Paris, 2003).

14 Lamb, in *Climate History and the Modern World*, takes the opposite position to Pascal Ascot and supports the theory of a 'warm' Roman Empire and a cooling at the beginning of the Middle Ages.

15 Bjorn Lomborg discusses these reserves in *The Sceptical Environmentalist: Measuring the Real State of the World* (Cambridge, 2001). See the chapter 'Global Warming', p. 262.

16 A chart of reconstructed temperatures for the period 1000–2000 appears in Bjorn Lomborg, *Sceptical Environmentalist*, p. 261.

17 Lamb, *Climate History and the Modern World*, p. 180.

18 Ascot, *Histoire du climat*. See also Emmanuel Le Roy Ladurie's commentary on this book: 'Famines, pollution et méteo', *Le Figaro Littéraire* (19 June 2003).

19 Fernand Braudel, *Civilisation matérielle, économie et capitalisme* (Paris, 1979),
vol. 1, p. 31. For climate in general and for Huntington's theories, see also
the collection *Ecrits sur l'histoire* (Paris, 1969), pp. 168–9 ('Y a-t-il une géographie de l'individu biologique?', article first published in 1944).

20 Trans. as Daniel S. Landes, *Richesse et pauvreté des nations* (Paris, 2000), pp.
23–39.

21 Leon Trotsky, *Littérature et revolution* (Paris, 1971), p. 285.

22 For Russian communism's grandiose projects, see Lucien Barnier, *A Quoi
rêvent les savants soviétiques* (Paris, 1958), particularly p. 42 for the projects
of the engineer Markine. I have dealt with this topic in my *La Mythologie
scientifique du communisme* (Paris, 2000), and have reproduced a brief
paragraph in the present text.

FIVE The Logic of the Flood

1 For the relationship between meteorology and mythology and religion,
I have consulted the articles by Jöelle Ducos, 'Le temps qu'il fait, signe de
Dieu ou du mal. La meteorology du Bourgeois de Paris', in *Le Mal et le
Diable: Leurs figures à la fin du Moyen Age*, ed. Nathalie Nabert (Paris,
1996), pp. 95–112, and 'Météorologie médiévale ou météorologie popu-
laire?', *La Météorologie*, special issue (April 1995), pp. 52–7. See also
Claude Thomasset and Jöelle Ducos, eds, *Le Temps qu'il fait au Moyen Age*
(Paris, 1998).

2 *Holy Bible* (King James version), Exodus 19: 16–19.

3 Ibid., Job 37: 11–13.

4 St Augustine, *The City of God*, 11, 33.

5 Ducos, 'Le temps qu'il fait', pp. 105–6.

6 For Charlemagne, see Eginhard, *Vita Caroli Magni*, 32. The information on
Etienne le Grand is drawn from the sixteenth-century Slavonic *Chronicle
of Moldavia*.

7 Rodulfus Glaber, *The Five Books of the Histories*, ed. and trans. John France
(Oxford, 1989), pp. 187–93.

8 In the following discussion, some of the information and interpretation
relating to the Flood and the apocalyptic imagination has been drawn
from my *La Fin du monde. Une histoire sans fin* (Paris, 1989 and 1999).

9 Voltaire, 'Déluge universel' in *Dictionnaire philosophique* (Paris, 1825),

vol. 2, pp. 526–32.

10 On the Flood tradition and its interpretations see Norman Cohn, *Noah's Flood, the Genesis Story in Western Thought* (New Haven and London, 1996).

11 *Oeuvres* of M. Boulanger, *L'Antiquité dévoilée par ses usages* (Amsterdam, 1778), vol. 3, pp. 268–70.

12 Ibid., vol. 1, pp. 11–15.

13 Georges Cuvier, *Discours sur les revolutions de la surface du globe* (Paris, 1825, 3rd edition), pp. 17–18.

14 Boucher de Perthes, *De l'homme antédiluvien et de ses oeuvres* (Paris, 1860), p. 78.

15 Louis Figuier, *La Terre avant le Déluge* (Paris, 1864), pp. 408–9.

16 See the examples of the universal histories published in England in the eighteenth century: *An Universal History from the Earliest Account of Time to the Present* (London, 1737) and *An Universal History from the Earliest Accounts to the Present* (London, 1779): the first dates the Flood in 2999, the second in 2348. In the nineteenth century, Cesare Cantu, the author of one of the most famous universal histories (*Storia universale*), went so far as to calculate the capacity of Noah's Ark as 42,413 tonnes. Even later, the Flood featured prominently in the work of certain authors, for example Marie-Nicolas Bouillet, in her *Atlas universel d'histoire et de géographie* (Paris, 1872, 2nd edition). In the chronology section, the creation of the world is dated at 5538 and the Flood at 3296.

17 Eduard Suess, *Das Antlitz der Erde* (Prague and Leipzig, 1885), vol. 1: 'Die Sintfluth', pp. 25–98.

18 C. Leonard Woolley, *Ur of the Chaldees* (London, 1929).

19 For hypotheses concerning the historicity of the Flood, see also Lloyd R. Bailey, *Noah, the Person and the Story in History and Tradition* (Columbia, 1989).

20 Polybius, *Histories*, 6, 5.

21 Lucretius, *De Rerum Natura*, end of book 2.

22 Seneca, *Quaestiones Naturales*, 3, 27–30.

23 On the end of antiquity–end of the world tandem, I refer the reader to my *La Fin du monde. Une histoire sans fin* (Paris, 1989 and 1999). See also Santo Mazzarino, *La Fine del mondo antico* (Milan, 1959).

24 Bede, *Ecclesiastical History of the English People*, ed. Bertram Congreve and R.A.B. Mynors (Oxford, 1969), book 1, chapter 32, p. 113.

25 A panorama of the fears of the time may be found in Jean Delumeau,

La Peur en Occident, XIV–XVIII siècles (Paris, 1978).

26 Pierre Bayle, *Dictionnaire historique et critique* (Amsterdam, 1720), vol. 3, article: 'Jean Stofler'.

27 Jean Bodin, *Les Six livres de la République*, book 4, chapter 2.

28 Maupertuis, *Oeuvres* (Dresden, 1752), 'Lettre sur la comète', pp. 183–206.

29 Laplace, *Exposition du système du monde* (1796), book 4, chapter 4: 'Des perturbations du mouvement elliptique des comètes'.

30 Gabriel Tarde, 'Fragment d'histoire future' in *Revue internationale de sociologie* (1896).

31 Alphonse Berget, 'La tremblements de Terre', *Je sais tout* (15 July 1905), pp. 698–704.

32 Camille Flammarion, Le Tremblement de terre de Messine', *Bulletin de la Société astronomique de France* (1909), p. 57.

33 Camille Flammarion, 'La Fin du monde', *Je sais tout* (15 February 1905), pp. 53–62.

34 'Le deluge de glace', *Journal des voyages et des aventures de terre et de mer* (19 January 1902).

six The Global Warming Dossier

1 For a more detailed analysis of the nuclear fear and other apocalyptic psychoses of the time, I refer the reader to my *La Fin du monde. Une histoire sans fin*, chapter 8 'Un monde en sursis?'

2 The 'nuclear winter' argument is summarized in Jonathan Schell, *The Abolition* (New York, 1984), particularly pp. 16–19.

3 Gordon Rattray Taylor, *The Doomsday Book* (Greenwich, CN, 1971), 'Ice Age or Heat Death?' pp. 55–75.

4 Jean-Marc Jancovici provides a detailed synthesis of the possible consequences of the most dramatic version of global warming in *L'Avenir climatique* (Paris, 2002).

5 Brian Fagan includes a complete climatological and historical dossier on El Niño in *Floods, Famines and Emperors: El Niño and the Fate of Civilizations* (New York, 1999).

6 Bjorn Lomborg, *The Sceptical Environmentalist: Measuring the Real State of the World* (Cambridge, 2001), 'Global Warming', pp. 258–324.

7 For the views of economists on global warming, see André Fourçans, *Effet*

de serre: le grand mensonge (Paris, 2002).

8 Studies published in *Science*, 14 February 2003 and *Nature*, 5 June 2003.

9 There is a good synthesis of the question in Olivier Postel-Vinay's 'Les Poles fondent-ils?', *La Recherche* (November 2002), pp. 34–43.

10 Pierre Kohler constructs a comprehensive dossier on anti-global warming arguments in *L'Imposture verte* (Paris, 2002), pp. 140–224.

11 The CO_2 emissions and global temperature curves from 1850 to 2000 are reproduced in Lomborg, *Sceptical Environmentalist*, pp. 260 and 263.

12 On the present state and tendencies of the poles, see 'The Icehouse Effect', *New Scientist* (1 June 2002).

13 The cooling thesis is argued by Yves Lenoir in *Climat de panique* (Lausanne, 2001). For the increase in some Antarctic glaciers and its interpretation, see Ian Joughin and Slawek Tulaczyk, 'Positive Mass Balance of the Ross Ice Streams, West Antarctica', *Science* (18 January 2002).

Index